D0928430

CAMPS
and
HOLIDAYS

by Elizabeth Robertson

For Guide and Ranger Guiders

Published by

The Girl Guides Association,
17-19 Buckingham Palace Road,
London, SW1W 0PT.

Price: 90p

First Published 1969

Second Edition 1970

Reprinted 1974

Reprinted 1975

Reprinted 1977

This book is the successor to *Campcraft* and is now the Girl Guides Association's manual for campers. It contains the same valuable information but embodies the new approach to camping needed by Guiders working on the Eight Point Programme.

Printed by

Wood Westworth & Co. Ltd.

St. Helens, Merseyside.

Contents

Chapter 1.

THE FUN OF GOING TO CAMP

Scouting began with a camp—on Brownsea Island. What an adventure it must have been, and what fun! Camping is, indeed, probably the finest legacy that B.-P. has left us, for where better than in camp can all that he gave us be practised? Camping has been described as 'the life-blood of Guiding', 'the crown of the year's activities', 'every girl's birthright as a Guide'—terms not too strong to indicate its place in our programme.

Ask any camper why she finds camping fun and she will find it difficult to answer. Hundreds of incidents, feelings, and memories combine to make the fun, yet, even if you could enumerate them all, there still remains an indefinable quality about camp—that quality that brings a light to the eyes of the girls when 'camp' is mentioned, that quality that draws together, in a closer bond, those who have shared the experience of camp.

What are some of the things, as far as they can be defined, that make camp fun?

Adventure

To the Guide the adventure of her first camp is in knowing what to do, but not quite knowing what it will be like; making plans in happy anticipation, and challenging herself to try something new. Or it is perhaps simply the adventure of leaving the shelter of home to go off with her friends, and learning to live out-of-doors with only a canvas roof above her and the wood she can find to cook her own meals; of using her hands to make herself comfortable and her eyes to appreciate the wonders around her. It is also the adventure of exploring new territory, finding people who have a different way of life, widening horizons physically and mentally. It is a spirit easily caught and carried on through life, adding zest to living.

> '*Go forth to seek; the quarry never found*
> *Is still a fever to the questing hound.*
> *The skyline is a promise—not a bound . . .*

said Masefield.

> '*Adventure on . . .*'

Achievement

To the Guide, creating a home for herself in a tent, cooking for herself and her friends, looking after herself—knowing that she is being trusted to do so—is fun. She may have cooked the sausages for the Patrol breakfast for the very first time, and all by herself. Perhaps she made a bridge or climbed a hill at dawn, though it was awful getting up so early. She may have learned to like tea, and had to put up the bedding rack three times before it was really firm enough . . . Camp offers countless opportunities to girls to try things they have never done, master skills, overcome fears, live up to the expectation of their Guiders, each achievement helping them to grow and giving them confidence in themselves.

Fellowship

There is no place where you can better 'see with the other fellow's eye in friendly sympathy', as B.-P. put it, than in camp. Friendships are made and deepened. The shared experiences bring the girls closer together so that they learn to understand each other and to be tolerant. In the Patrol and in the Ranger group the shy, diffident girl, even the 'difficult' girl, finds herself accepted, because of the contribution she has to make, because the unit is small enough for her to matter, and she blossoms as a result. A shared difficulty, a hilarious activity, a quiet moment round the Camp-Fire in the twilight, can break down barriers and give the feeling of belonging. Guider and Guide in such a situation grow closer in understanding in a way that only the atmosphere of camp can bring about. How much can be gained from such mutual trust and understanding!

Awareness

Life in camp brings out much more than an awareness of surroundings and of other people. For the girls there emerges an added awareness of themselves, as people who can do things and are accepted by others, and the joy that that feeling brings. There is space and silence to think and become aware, if only vaguely at first, of the beauty and wonder of nature, of God its Creator, and of God's part in their lives. It can be the opportunity for them to see more clearly how the Promise can be at the heart of all life. In camp it is good to be alive—an attitude you find reflected in the eyes of the girls and in their little unexpected thoughtful acts.

Making It Fun

'Some people', said B.-P. 'are so busy organising their camp that they have got home before they have begun to enjoy it'. The secret of success is to learn how to make a camp, not as an all-consuming activity in itself, but as a base simply for adventure and fun.

The following chapters do not give the pattern for a camp. There is no set pattern; each camp is what the girls make it. It is a book of suggestions on how things can be done, how things can be organised, but above all, how to ensure a satisfying programme, how to ensure that the camp is fun for everyone.

The Guider's task? To train herself, to train her Unit, and especially to give them, and herself, the opportunity to enjoy the many benefits and pleasures of camp.

Chapter 2.

DIFFERENT TYPES OF CAMP

This chapter deals simply with the basic principles of different types of camp. Details of running the camps will appear in subsequent chapters.

The type of camp you choose will, of course, depend on the age group involved, and on what will make the best base for the chosen activities of your group.

Standing Camps

This type of camp is the most popular with the Guide Section and is perhaps the best, as younger Guides will feel more secure if they have a fixed base or home to return to. Generally tents and equipment are of the heavier type, and the camp may last anything from a week-end to a fortnight. Numbers generally do not exceed that of a Guide Company. For larger camps see page 11.

Ideally the Company camps in Patrols, each Patrol being an independent unit, with its own camp, and making its own meals in its own kitchen. (The evening hot drink and hot water for personal washing may be provided centrally.) Chores at a camp run in this way have an obvious purpose (no wood—no fire—no dinner!), meals are quickly prepared, and served hot and speedily. Above all, the Patrol has a wonderful opportunity to work together as a unit, while, at the same time, individuals have much more opportunity to progress in all of the Eight Points of the Guide programme. 'Patrol camping is the logical outcome of the full use of the Patrol System' (*A Handbook for Guiders—Guide Section*). Even when Patrols have to be made up artificially, as in a District or Division camp, the girls become much more quickly integrated when Patrol camping. Rangers in standing camps may also wish to divide into Patrol-sized groups if this fits in best with their camp programme.

There may be some camps, e.g., a Service camp or Interest camp, where it is found more convenient to camp as a Company and cook meals centrally, with perhaps extra staff to allow more time to be spent on the project on hand.

The Patrol Camp

A Patrol Leader gaining her Patrol Camp Permit may take her Patrol to camp under certain conditions. This camp is rather like a single unit of a standing camp, and indeed a girl who is used to Patrol camping with her Company will take her Permit in her stride. Hints for the Patrol Camp Permit are given in *The Guide Handbook* along with the requirements and conditions.

Lightweight Camps

Ranger Guides, in particular, enjoy lightweight camping. They can indulge in the holiday of their choice with cheap bed and board (the lightweight equipment giving them much more freedom of movement) and all the additional fun of learning to make themselves comfortable in small tents, and of being completely independent.

Camps may be with a Guider or Rangers may go on their own. Conditions attached to running such camps will be found in the Ranger and Ranger Guider's Handbooks.

Numbers will probably be smaller than in Guide camps, and generally these camps are of shorter duration. Longer lightweight camps need at least a few experienced campers. So break in your

Rangers with a few week-ends and they will enjoy the longer camp all the more.

These lightweight camps may be 'base' camps to allow the Rangers to take part in some chosen project or projects—pioneering, painting, photography, ski-ing in the Cairngorms, pony-trekking, service to the community, to the National Trust, etc. *The Ranger Guide Handbook* will give them plenty of 'starters'.

Lightweight camps may also be mobile camps—exploring new country, a historical trail, etc.—and various means of transport may take the Rangers' fancy: pony, canoe, foot, cycle, scooter, car, minibus.

Cooking arrangements will, of course, be made to suit each individual situation (see Chapter 5).

Overnight Camps

Your Rangers will enjoy setting off with a tent and all they need for a night, and overnight camping is popular with those who cannot fix holidays to fit in with Unit camp plans. Older Guides, too, enjoy overnight hikes on occasions, as a foretaste of pleasures to come when they are Rangers. (For conditions see the Handbooks.)

A minimum of three is recommended for such a camp, especially when camping off the beaten track.

Guiders' Camps

These can be an excellent opportunity for Guiders to 'recharge batteries' or simply to learn about the joys of camping.

While camp is the natural place to learn camp skills, it is important to see that the fun of camp for a new Guider is not spoiled by an overdose of instruction in skills.

The Guiders' camp will be most enjoyable for all if the atmosphere is informal and relaxed. Cooking in groups of four to six allows for greater freedom and informality as well as giving Guiders the 'feel' of Patrol camping.

Ideally, all taking part plan the camp, and neither programme nor menu need be a pattern for Guide camps, but can cater for more adult tastes and pockets.

Very Large Camps

In general large camps should be avoided, as the individual and her needs are lost in the crowd. If numbers are much above 36, it is better to divide into groups with a Guider in charge of each. If a camp of over 50 is planned, consult your District Commissioner, as special permission is needed.

For a special occasion, however, a Country or Region may want to organise a larger gathering, e.g., an International Camp. This can be a very valuable experience, but do get permission first. Such a camp needs detailed organisation.

A County or Division may also feel it would be a valuable experience to bring together Patrols from different Companies, each camping as an individual unit and being self-supporting. It is a good idea to divide such a camp into groups with a Guider attached to each, so that each individual can feel she is known.

Camping with Boys

Camping with Scouts and other Youth Groups can be a very valuable experience for Rangers and older Guides.

The Venture Scout programme is very much in line with the Guide Eight Point Programme and Rangers and Venture Scouts will find much common ground on which to base joint training and activities. These in turn may well lead to a request for a joint camp. An Education Authority course in some outdoor pursuit may also inspire the participants to arrange a joint camp or similar residential venture as a follow-up. Orienteering, pioneering, canoeing, sailing, pot-holing, mountaineering are just a few of the activities which might form the basis for a joint camp.

A joint camp may also provide the base from which some chosen service project may be carried out. It may be a project devised by themselves, e.g. a particular service to a community, such as clearing of ground, laying a nature trail, or they may wish to participate in some nationally or internationally sponsored Youth Service project.

To be a success, a joint camp should have a definite purpose, clearly defined. Careful planning at all levels is essential. Permission must be obtained through the appropriate Commissioner in the first place, as it is obvious that such a camp must be carefully supervised by responsible adults of both sexes. It would take only one irresponsibly-run joint camp to bring the whole Movement into disrepute, quite apart from the harm to individuals involved.

The actual planning and running of the camp, however, should be, as far as possible, the responsibility of the girls and boys concerned. If they know that they are being trusted to see that all is well, they will respond to that trust and probably achieve a higher standard than that set by an imposed discipline.

Those responsible for planning the programme must ensure that it is a full one with emphasis on activities other than purely social ones. They should also see to it that, wherever possible and practical, the participants in a joint camp share in appropriate preliminary training, so that the camp comes as the climax of a shared project and is not just an isolated event.

The site for a joint camp must be chosen with a view to providing well-separated sleeping quarters and toilet facilities. The groups will, of course, share in camp chores, meals, etc. It is essential to have a definite time agreed on for 'back to own camps'.

A great deal of good can come from a well-run joint camp. Boys and girls who normally meet only on a social basis gain a new and healthy respect for each other, as they discover unsuspected talents in each other, and a healthy 'camaraderie' develops from interests shared and difficulties overcome together.

Chapter 3

PREPARING FOR CAMP

'When we go to camp we'll . . .' This sort of phrase, cropping up at regular intervals, is one of the best bits of preparation you can make for camp, as it builds up the thinking of your Unit towards camp and shows camp in its rightful place as the natural highlight of your Guide year. However, there are many other preparations you have to make for camp, both practical and inspirational, and this chapter deals with both.

First, however, before embarking on preparations, do check on your camping qualifications. (See the Handbooks or *P.O.R.*) Your Commissioner will be able to help you, and will arrange training if needed. The Guide Movement has often been praised for ensuring, as it does, that girls in camp are in charge of responsible people who have proved that they are capable of caring for the health and well-being of a number of girls under camp conditions. This means a great deal to parents.

It is wise to start planning well in advance, especially from the point of view of getting the site you want, and of hiring tents during a popular camping time. The girls, too, will want to include preparations for camp in their Patrol and Company programmes. This does not mean, however, that a last minute inspiration, a few phone calls, and an 'eleventh-hour' camp will not be a success. On the contrary, with experienced campers this may well prove to be the best camp ever, and to bear the mark of success that attends any event which is the outcome of enthusiasm combined with a sense of responsibility.

The Site

Deciding Where to Go

Your Patrol Leaders' or Rangers' Council will no doubt have plenty of ideas about this, depending on what they hope their main ploys in camp will be. With a Company new to camping, or with limited experience of it, it will probably be wiser for you to offer them alternatives from which to choose. The Handbooks give ideas to work on. Otherwise they may be tempted to choose something too ambitious or opt for 'the same as last year'. What matters is that the choice is theirs in the end.

Rangers have an even wider variety of possibilities, and within the Ranger group there may be widely differing suggestions. The wise Guider, rather than offer comment or advice, will ask a few judicious questions. How much will it cost? Can we get there and back in time? etc., thereby bringing over-ambitious plans into proportion, and cutting down the alternatives, but at the same time leaving the choice in the Rangers' hands.

Whatever the Section, the girls must feel, from the start, that it is *their* camp in every way and not something laid on by adults.

Finding the Site

How do you go about finding the actual site? One of the best sources of information is what one might call 'The Guide Grapevine', i.e. hearing about a good site from other Guiders you meet at District, Division, or County gatherings, or at a Training Centre. With the name and address of the 'source' in your notebook you have a head-start on the information you will need if you decide on the site. So keep asking and listening whenever Guiders are around.

Your Guides or Rangers, with access to their own 'grapevines' and perhaps those of the Scouts, may also be able to suggest some sites.

Finding your own site by means of personal exploration is very rewarding—by chance when on holiday, or on an expedition with Patrol Leaders or Rangers for the specific purpose, or on a day out with other Guiders. Before you go ahead with arrangements make sure any site you find is approved by the local C.A., as she will know of any snags.

If a site is still not forthcoming, you can write enquiring for one to the Camp Adviser of the area of your choice (your own Camp Adviser will be able to give you the name and address). Be sure to give details of what you have in mind, your approximate numbers and dates, and enclose a stamped, addressed envelope.

If you have enquired about a site and find you do not want it, be sure to write and say so, at once, so that others can have the chance of it.

Information about sites available can also be found in *Guider*, including those at the Guide Training Centres and the C.H.Q. sites at Blackland, Ynysgain, and Brownsea Island.

For mobile camps it may not be necessary or practicable to have sites previously arranged. Over-organisation could kill the adventure of such a camp, but the safety and welfare of the girls must be considered carefully before leaving too much to chance. The advice of the Camp Adviser and others who have gone before should be sought. Rangers may, of course, choose to use public camp-sites and this can be a valuable experience as well as a means of reducing equipment.

Wherever and whenever you camp, permission must be obtained from the owner of the site. Common sense, common courtesy, and the good name of the Guide Movement demand it.

What to Look For in a Site

Sites are unfortunately 'born' rather than 'made', so that the ideal site is hard to find. However, a 'camp-site eye' is something that is quickly acquired (and fun to use when travelling anywhere).

General Impression. The general look of the spot is the first item for consideration. It must be in an attractive setting, with preferably an attractive view—a place that looks good even on a bad day! (That was B.-P's idea, too!) Unfortunately, however, that is not enough. Various practical considerations must be studied.

Size. There must obviously be room and sufficient level ground for all the tents, etc., required.

Soil. The following notes may help:

Sandy soil drains well, but, if the site is exposed, extra long pegs may be needed.

Gravel drains well and holds pegs well.

Loam (blackish soil) has reasonably good drainage and peg holdage.

Chalk (grey-white) has poorish drainage.

Clay is liable to be water-logged; peg holdage is poor and digging hard.

Rock drainage on the whole is good.There must be sufficient subsoil to hold pegs. There are obvious digging difficulties.

Peat is absorbent, peg holdage is poor, and there is danger of fire spreading underground.

BEWARE OF:

Rushes and cotton grass: usually wet and boggy.
Long grass: wet in mornings, tough digging.
A dip in the ground: gets very wet after rain.
Land immediately downhill from farm buildings: insanitary.
Low lying ground near river: flooding.

Water. A safe drinking water supply should be readily available (remembering that pails of water are heavy). If a site is to be used often it may be worth while having water piped to the site for the season.

Tap water must be checked to see that the supply is from the mains.

Lakes, rivers, wells, and springs are unsuitable for drinking.

Hillside streams and springs are generally wholesome, but check that there is no source of pollution upstream.

If in doubt at all, boil rapidly for at least five minutes all water used for consumption.

For smaller camps water purifying tablets may be obtained from chemists or camping stores. These are useful, too, for mobile and overnight camps.

If transport is available and there is a supply of washing water near the site, it may be possible to collect a daily supply of drinking water in polythene water carriers with caps, provided the benefits of the site justify such an operation.

Wood. If cooking is to be done on wood fires, there must be a sufficient supply of dead wood near at hand. It is essential to ensure you have permission to gather wood, and it is also advisable, when assessing your needs in this direction, to find out if anyone will be using the site before you. The type of wood available is also important. Bad burning wood will lead to smoke-begotten tears and frustration, while feeding the fire a perpetual diet of fir or other resinous woods will also create tricky, though less acute problems.

Accessibility. For a standing camp, with its fairly heavy equipment, there must be some means of conveying the equipment to the site. If the lorry or bus cannot get near, perhaps a friendly tractor will oblige. Otherwise the disadvantages of having to manhandle equipment some distance will have to be weighed very carefully against the benefits of the site, and the participants fully informed of the situation in advance. The problem of getting stores to camp comes into this too. If a car is not available, account will need to be taken of whether it is possible to have stores delivered and whether vans will call.

Exposure. A site should be sheltered from the prevailing wind (the shape of the trees will indicate this) and should get plenty of sunshine. It is annoying to find that a site, visited one sunny morning, gets not a blink after 2 p.m.

Solid shelter. It is wise, especially with inexperienced campers, to arrange for some solid shelter to be available nearby, should the weather become impossible. This may be a barn, a local school, or hall. More experienced Companies may be prepared to make do with a marquee (though this can be more of a liability on a very exposed site). Smaller camps with experienced campers may feel they do not require such shelter.

An impossible list? The consoling thing is that generally someone has gone before and can pass on all the information about snags and how to overcome them. The new camper would be advised to go to a tried site not too far from home, but for the experienced camper and her Unit, there is a tremendous thrill in pioneering a new site.

If at all possible visit the site.

Here is a handy check list:

Study state of ground, shelter, etc.

Check on water supply.

Obtain permission to light fires, cut turf, gather wood.
Find out about where you may walk, game preserves, etc.
Find someone to dig, if required.
Find tractor transport, if required.
Check that you will not be sharing the site with farm animals. (Cows are unpleasant bedfellows.)
Find out the correct postal address.
Check the position of the nearest telephone.
Find out about delivery vans, milk rounds, shopkeepers and any other information required by the Quartermaster.
Find out the name and address and phone number of the doctor.
Find out the local places and times of worship and contact the ministers.
Above all, study the possibilities for adventure, activities, pioneering, exploration, study of local history, culture, natural history, etc., and make a sketch map for your Unit. Any information you can pass on to them will help them in planning their camp.

Equipment

The ideal situation is for each Unit to have its own equipment. Apart from cutting down the cost of camp, the girls will take great pride in keeping it in good condition before, at, and after camp, and both derive satisfaction and learn many new skills in doing so. Equipment will also be available for practice.

Patrols enjoy raising money to acquire their own kitchen equipment and will cherish it fondly when it is their own hard-won property. Rangers, too, will enthusiastically gather together lightweight equipment and will be far keener to get out and use it than if it has to be borrowed or hired each time. The very exercise of acquiring camp equipment, whether by making it or raising money to buy it will help many girls to progress in some of the Eight Points of the programme.

Equipment should be checked, with a time margin for replacement or repair. This is a responsibility which can be handed over to the girls according to their experience and interest.

Companies who have not yet acquired equipment may have District, Division, or County equipment available at a small charge. Often a rota system for first choice of dates is in operation, so the availability of equipment should be checked early to avoid disappointment. There is also the possibility of using an equipped site either at a Training Centre or belonging to a County. (Many are advertised in *Guider*.) To avoid subsequent disappointment, check carefully how many campers can be accommodated.

If equipment has to be hired commercially, check the reliability of the firm. (The C.A. may be able to help you in this.) Book early, especially if camping at a popular time. It may be possible to come to an arrangement with others using the site to take over or hand over equipment to cut down transport costs.

Equipment List

A list of equipment which may possibly be required for standing camps follows.

Tents (see Chapter 4).
- Sleeping tents
- Store tent
- **Spare tent, if possible, for first aid, etc.**
- Marquee (optional)

Kitchen equipment (See Chapter 5 for details).

Sanitation, etc. (See Chapter 6).
- Toilet cubicles (one per 8 at least—ideally one per Patrol) with furnishings
- Wash cubicles (one per 8 at least—ideally one per Patrol) with basins
- Hot water boiler
- Buckets
- Extra blankets
- First aid outfit
- Incinerator if required

Groundsheets. One sleeping groundsheet (1·8m. × ·9m.) per Guide, plus one extra per tent and a few spares. (Guides should bring their own individual 'sitter' groundsheets but a few spare ones may be brought for visitors.)

Miscellaneous:

Flagpole (unless poles available near site)
Colours
Spare rope and string
Spare pegs
Spade
Saw
Hand axe (0·5 kg. head)
Noticeboard if required
Drawing pins
Hammer, nails, and pliers
Lamp or large torch
Items based on programme, e.g., rope for pioneering projects, maps of the area, compasses.
Books and materials for camp activities.
Books on the following subjects are useful: local history, birds, flowers, trees, photography, pioneering, etc.
Books of readings and prayers.
Drawing paper, felt pens, etc.

Some Notes on the Use and Care of this Equipment

Axe. Must be of a reliable make and sharp. A blunt one is more dangerous than a sharp one, as it can glance off a log. The

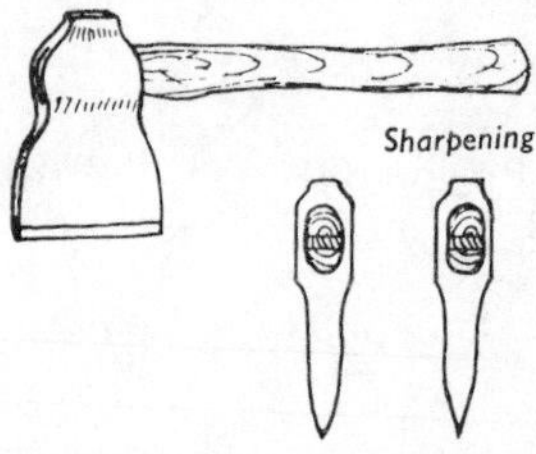

Fig. 1 *Incorrect* *Correct*

Fig 2

head should be well tapered and the handle should have a comfortable grip (Fig. 1). Before using an axe, be sure that the head is firmly wedged in the shaft. If it is loose, put the axe head down and hit the end of the shaft with a mallet. Hit the wedge firmly in.

Grease the head (not the wood) to protect it and immerse for at least 24 hours in water to swell the wood. When not in use an axe should be kept in its sheath or with the edge embedded in a tree stump or block of wood (Fig. 2). No Guide should be allowed to use an axe unless she has first had successful supervised instruction and knows the following rules:

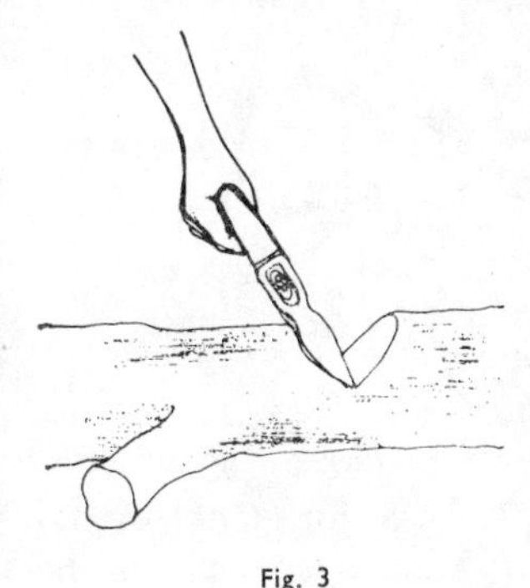

Fig. 3

Make sure no one is near enough to be hurt by flying sticks.

Rest the stick or log against wood and chop against this wood, not over the air.

Keep legs well clear of the line of swing.

Chop through thick logs by making a notch, hitting alternately from right and left (Fig. 3).

Thinner ones can be chopped at an angle.

Hold the axe at the end of the shaft, swing it well up, then let the weight of the axe bring it down. Practise until you feel that it is the axe that is doing the work, not you.

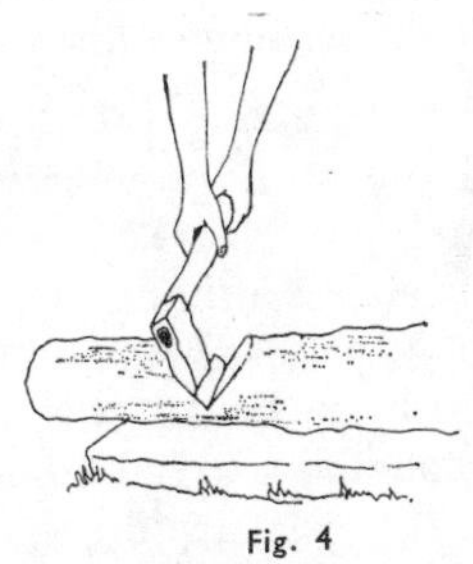

Fig. 4

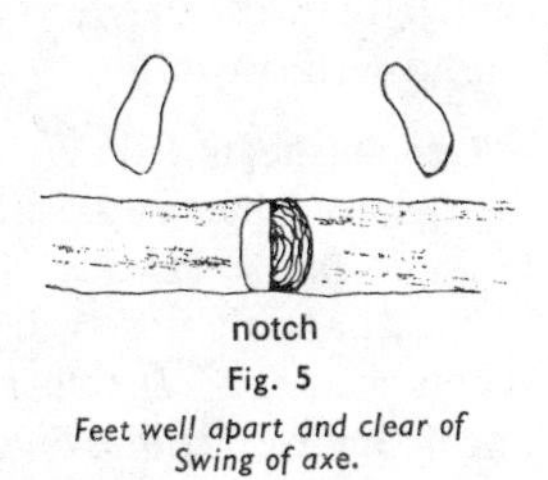

Fig. 5

Feet well apart and clear of Swing of axe.

Saw. A small pruning saw with coarse, widely-spaced teeth is specially good. A small bushman's saw is useful if there is large wood to cut. This can be used by two Guides, each one pulling only towards herself, or when used by one can be held between heels and knees and the wood drawn up and down against it (Fig. 6). A chain saw is useful when weight is a problem. For gadgets a Junior Hack-saw is practical, but it is wise to have a few spare blades. The saw should be kept sharp. (This is a job for an expert.) Both it and the axe should be thoroughly dried and greased before storing.

Points to remember when sawing:

Wood to be sawn should be raised and sawn over air.

The whole blade of the saw should be used.

The backstroke is the effective one.

Knots in the wood should be avoided.

Fig. 6

Spade. A light garden spade is best for Guides and the cutting edge should be kept sharp. The spade should be cleaned after use. If the ground is known to be difficult, a small entrenching tool can be used, or a pick-axe borrowed locally. Stack sods grass to grass and soil to soil and remember to water daily, and when filling in a pit make the level of the top a little higher than the original to allow for the settling of the earth, and stamp well down.

Groundsheets. P.V.C. is one of the most popular materials for groundsheets, as it is light and durable. Rubber coating tends to perish readily, and proofed canvas, although very tough, is heavier, difficult to dry, and tends to become smelly. Groundsheets must be kept clean. Spilt food in particular (which should not be near a groundsheet anyway) should be wiped immediately. Care should be taken to avoid contact with sharp objects, stones, etc., and anything hot. Before camp check groundsheets for holes by holding them up to the light (or in the case of canvas by placing them on wet grass and kneeling on them to see if damp comes through). Where a repair can be made, this is best done with a stick-on waterproof material. Groundsheets should not be stored folded; they will readily crack or perish where the folds have been. When dry they should be hung over rounded bars, or rolled.

Equipment for Lightweight Camps

Rangers will work out their own modifications for lightweight camps, depending on circumstances.

Lightweight tents can often be borrowed privately or from Scouts, but always put them up before setting off to check that no vital piece is missing, and also to see that you know how. Half dark and howling gale are not the best conditions for learning tent pitching! Other items for lightweight camps, such as stoves, rucksacks, etc., can often be borrowed until you have acquired your own.

Groundsheets of nylon-coated P.V.C. are best if money can be spared, as they are light and can be folded very small. Buckets and basins of canvas or oilskin are light to carry, and fold flat.

Down or terylene-filled sleeping bags are usually lightest to carry, and the number of blankets can be reduced by wearing a woolly, and a scarf round the waist. A very light inner sleeping bag can be knitted with scraps of four-ply wool (Shetland wool is warmest). Cast on about 100 stitches on large needles (approx. size 1). Knit until the piece is twice the length you require, then fold and sew up loosely at the sides. Other suggestions for light-weight equipment have been mentioned throughout the book, but it is more fun to do your own weight-reducing.

For mobile camps special preparations, depending on the mode of transport, will have to be made.

On foot. Cut the weight down to the minimum (4–6 kg. per person, including tent, utensils, etc. is reasonable) by taking only the quantity required packed in lightweight containers (e.g., put the exact amount of coffee required in a light plastic container instead of carrying the tin or jar) and by sharing items whenever possible (provided it is hygienic).

Rucksacks should be comfortable to carry and packed so that the weight is evenly distributed—not all at the bottom or to one side. A high pack rucksack is best for this. Shoulder pads of foam rubber may prevent chafing.

Correct footwear is essential. For hills, climbing or hill-walking boots, depending on the nature of the activity, must be worn. (Choose half a size larger than normal footwear to allow for thick socks.) For walking on the level, boots, as above, or strong walking shoes should be worn. Smooth leather soles are unsuitable for rough ground. Thin-soled or slip-on shoes will soon cause considerable discomfort. Gym shoes are unsuitable for walking but are useful to change into, when on the camp-site. The uppers of boots should be kept supple (castor oil is good for this) and a waterproofing wax should be applied regularly. Two pairs of socks give greatest comfort—a thin pair next to the feet, preferably of wool or wool and cotton mixture, with a thick woollen pair on top. Footwear should be 'broken in' and practice walks for this organised. Feet can be hardened for walking if they are rubbed regularly with methylated or surgical spirit.

Clothing should be light but warm, cotton and wool being better than synthetic materials which do not absorb perspiration. Devise a system of layers which can be added to or removed according to the temperature. Test out clothing, especially shorts and jeans, for chafing beforehand. For hill and mountain walking, especially, really warm and windproof clothing is essential; as well as adequate protection from rain. A change of clothing is vital. Expert guidance should be sought on measures to take to prevent 'exposure' on hill, mountain, and moorland expeditions.

On cycle. Cycles must be checked carefully (local police are usually willing to help over this). The height of the saddle should be adjusted, if necessary, to allow the ball of the foot to reach the pedal comfortably.

Weight of kit should be reduced to the minimum as described in the section 'On foot' above. Kit is best packed in correct pannier bags on either side of the back wheel with the weight evenly distributed. Although a cycle basket attached to the handlebars is useful, it should not be packed with heavy items.

It is wise to practise cycling with a heavy load, as this can affect the control of a cycle, particularly when going downhill or round corners. Several long cycle runs are advisable, in advance, to prepare the 'anatomy' for the unaccustomed use.

Clothing should be comfortable and light (see section 'On foot' above). A windproof anorak or jacket is an essential item and a waterproof cycling cape offers the best protection from rain. Shorts are practical for cycling. Stockings and jeans are unsuitable for cycling in wet weather.

On pony. Seek expert advice on the best means of carrying equipment if this form of transport is used. Riding practice is advisable to prepare the 'anatomy' and check the comfort of clothing (which should include a riding hat).

By car or minibus. It is advisable to have a trial loading to make sure there is room for the participants to travel in comfort. Reduce the bulk as far as possible. If using a roof-rack, reserve for it the lighter items, well-protected from the rain, securely fastened with no loose covers (which will flap noisily). Ensure that the weight of luggage on the rack does not exceed the recommended maximum and is not unevenly distributed, otherwise the performance of the vehicle may be adversely, possibly dangerously, affected.

The vehicle should, of course, be carefully checked. Ensure, too, that it has the appropriate insurance cover and that the driver has the requisite qualifications. If driving in remote areas or abroad, it may be wise to carry a spare-part kit, which garages often supply on a 'sale or return' basis.

Transport

For standing camps this is a big item and should also be booked well in advance. Your District 'Guide grapevine' will usually be able to advise you on the best and cheapest transport available locally.

Some bus firms are prepared to take equipment and kit as well as bodies and, by serving a dual purpose, often work out cheapest. A 45-seater bus will take equipment, kit, and up to 30 campers, without discomfort.

If sending equipment by train, find out from your local station the best and cheapest way to ensure your equipment arrives on time. For this means of transport special care is needed in packing and tying up.

Furniture van, cattle float, lorry, private cars (make sure the poles will go in), may be your best choice (but do make sure that their insurance covers journeys with people). It is often worthwhile to obtain a few estimates before deciding. The girls themselves may not, by law, travel on an open lorry or on a tractor bogie.

If you have control over the timing of your transport it is usually a good idea to arrive about midday or early afternoon (taking a packed lunch) and leave about the same time or a little later.

Finance

As the factors involved in assessing the actual cost of a camp differ so considerably, no realistic figures can be given. This will have to be assessed on such things as:

Hiring of tents, or contribution towards wear and tear of own equipment.
Transport—both people and equipment.
Food and other items required.
Any planned activities which require financial support or special equipment.
Fee for site and any local expenses (digging, etc.).
Tips.
Guiders' petrol (fetching stores).
Postages, phone calls, etc.

Your first camp will be most difficult to assess, but you will get valuable help in this from more experienced Guiders or from your C.A. Thereafter it is a help (and not only for finance) to keep all your camp records, bills, etc., till next camp.

Many Guides like paying for their camp by means of a saving

scheme and cards can be issued to them for this. This money should be put in a Savings Bank, thus gaining interest. In order to avoid carrying a large sum of money to camp, Guiders who have a Current Account at a Bank may want to transfer this money—duly receipted—to their account and pay camp bills by cheque. Many Guiders find it a good idea, too, to have a deposit from intending campers, not returnable after a certain date.

Your Company may want to plan a money raising effort for a specially expensive camp, e.g., if transport or hiring costs are high, or if you plan some project which requires money. Generally, however, each girl should pay a realistic fee for her camp. Something for nothing is usually not appreciated. In cases of real hardship there are often special funds which can help. Your Commissioner will be able to guide you about this or may approach your Local Association for help for you.

The Company, in planning the camp, will, of course, take into consideration the funds available and the amount the girls are prepared to pay. If economies have to be made these should not result in inadequate food. It is cheaper for everyone if you provide plenty of good, wholesome food, and forbid the more expensive parental parcels of sweets sent to supplement an inadequate diet!

A camp that makes a large profit (beyond a fair margin for wear and tear of equipment) is *not* a success financially.

Camp Staff

What? For a Guide standing camp, the minimum requirements are three responsible adults, one of whom must have the appropriate qualifications and the others should have camped before. One staff member per ten Guides is a reasonable minimum. Generally one Guider is responsible for catering and another for health, but in a small camp there can be some doubling up.

The staffing of Ranger camps will depend very much on the type of camp being run and the experience and age of the Rangers. (Fifteen-year-olds will require more supervision than seventeen-year-olds). A decision as to minimum requirements should be based on common sense and a sense of responsibility, and should be made in consultation with the Commissioner and C.A.

Where? Sometimes a Guider has difficulty in finding sufficient staff. This can be overcome, very happily, perhaps, if a Guider brings children and/or husband where suitable arrangements can be made for accommodating them on the site. Often a Brownie Guider will enjoy coming to camp, and may not have thought of it till you ask her—Commissioners, too! Students who have been keen campers as Guides or Rangers but have not time to continue with Guiding at the moment, are often delighted to come, and it is also a good way of keeping them in touch with Guiding until they are free again. Older Rangers and Young Leaders also make excellent assistants. Care must be taken, however, not to use them just as 'dogs-bodies'! Lastly, non-Guide friends (whether brought along 'thin edge of the wedge-wise' or not) may prove to be very valuable helpers with their fresh approach and unhidebound ideas.

It is helpful if as many of the staff as possible can keep in touch with the girls when the latter are planning the camp, so that any practical preparations can be made to fit in with the activities they have in mind.

Co-operating with Parents

Parents of girls who have never camped before may well be a little apprehensive about allowing their daughters to go to camp, so it is vital to make a point of seeing parents, acquainting them of the safeguards, and answering any of their queries. It is natural, too, that they will want to meet the person who is to be in charge of their daughter and have an opportunity to discuss health matters. Doubtful parents will have added confidence if they see that arrangements are being made in a business-like way. So you would do well to issue a kind of prospectus or information sheet to parents, giving such things as dates, travel arrangements, correct postal address, cost, pocket money allowed, when visitors will be welcome, Guider's address and phone number. This may be combined with a Permission to Camp form which Guiders, in their own interests, are advised to have signed by parents. Pads of these forms are on sale at Guide shops, but a Guider who is acquainted with an accommodating duplicator may prefer to draw up her own. (It is useful to keep one copy as a guide for next year.) At the same time kit lists (pads of which are also on sale in Guide shops) can be issued and any queries about them answered.

A Suggested Kit List for a Guide Camp

Kit should be carried in a kitbag, grip, or rucksack, not a suitcase, and should be named.

Bedding should be wrapped in some waterproof material and securely tied.

Dishes and cutlery should be in a drawstring bag.

Complete uniform (In some cases it may prove more practical to take only camp uniform)
Strong walking shoes
Raincoat (plastic, nylon, or oilskin)
Official camp dress (many Companies keep a stock of these)
Blue shirt or T-shirt, and navy shorts
Jersey (navy)
Jeans (navy)
Anorak (navy or blue)
Gumboots
Plimsolls
Sleeping bag and/or blankets
Warm pyjamas and old jersey and woollen socks
Small pillow or air pillow
Complete changes of underclothes
Spare socks
Toilet kit and towel
Old plastic mac (a discarded one for camp wear in wet weather)
Sitter groundsheet (a square of plastic—usually second-hand)
Notepaper and stamped envelopes
Notebook and pencil
Dishcloth and tea towel
Bowl, plate, mug (unbreakable)
Knife, fork, dessert spoon, teaspoon
Apron
Handkerchiefs

Per Patrol: Badge, belt, shoe cleaning kit, clothes brush, mirror, compass, ball of string, sewing kit, pocket first aid kit, haversack.

Rangers will modify such a list according to type of camp, weight requirements, etc.

Insurance

Guiders within the U.K. and Ulster taking Units to camp are covered by the *Guiders Indemnity Policy*, the premium being paid by C.H.Q. This means that Guiders are protected against legal claims arising from accidents to individuals in their care or from damage caused by those in their care. All members within the U.K. are also insured by C.H.Q. under the *Personal Accident and Medical Policy* which provides various benefits over and above those supplied by the National Health Service. Details are available in the leaflet *What Every Guider Should Know about Insurance* and also appear at intervals in *Guider*. The Guider should notify C.H.Q. immediately if an accident, where such insurance may operate, occurs in camp.

Camp Forms

Your Commissioner will be able to obtain from the C.A. the form required before you take the girls to camp. This is a simple form of control, so that those in charge of camping in the County will know who and how many are camping where and when. A small camp fee is usually payable, to defray the expenses involved in administering camping, visiting camps, etc. You should find out how long before camp this form should be sent in.

Preparations in the Unit

The bigger the share the girls can take in all camp preparations the better. Guides and Rangers throughout the winter or in the months preceding camp will be preparing for some of their proposed camp ploys or activities. Maps of the area and a detailed map of the site are essential, and ideally there should be a visit to the site by the P.L.s or some of the Rangers. Books about the area, if available, are invaluable. The girls will also be acquiring skills they will require: anything from making plaster casts to taking good photographs.

Rangers, individually and collectively, and Guides in their Patrols will also be preparing by acquiring the camp skills they will need, and this may form part of the Company or Patrol meeting time. Guides will find a great deal of help in their Handbooks. The Guider can often help by obtaining the necessary equipment with which to practise, e.g., tent, screening, flagpole.

The wise Guider will, of course, find adequate opportunity to train her Patrol Leaders in the necessary camp skills according to their needs, which will differ from Company to Company and even within a Company. The success of a camp run in Patrols depends very largely on the camping knowledge of the P.L. and her ability to lead a Patrol successfully.

As well as preparing their personal kit, Rangers will be busy preparing lightweight equipment, and Guides will enjoy making Patrol equipment. This will give many added opportunities of developing skills and adding new ones. New recipes will be collected and suggestions made for the camp menu. Many may make an effort to become more physically fit for camp, especially if a strenuous programme is planned.

Rangers should buy or borrow books or specialist magazines on the chosen activities (see Appendix and *The Ranger Guide Handbook* for a few suggestions) and seek local expert advice on skills, equipment, clothing, etc., required. The winter's programme can then be built round the proposed camp and might include such things as map-reading, learning how to walk or climb, cycle or car maintenance, local history, architecture, inn-signs, and weatherlore. It would be extremely foolish to attempt any sort of camp without adequate physical, mental, and purely practical preparation.

Any activities which help the girls to be more aware of their surroundings, to cultivate an adventurous spirit, to become a really integrated Patrol or Ranger group, to co-operate well with others (the Handbooks are full of suggestions for this), will contribute greatly to the success of any camp to come.

Above all, encourage anything at all which will help the girls to feel that it is really their camp, run by themselves. You are just going to be there!

The Guider in Charge

What are your own personal preparations?

Unflagging enthusiasm of the kind that acts as a booster to that of the Guides and Rangers and not the over-riding, 'bull-dozer' variety.

Knowledge of the girls in your charge, so that you can see that their needs are being fulfilled. If taking Guides other than your own, try to meet them beforehand and find out something of them from their Guider.

A notebook, with all the facts, figures, addresses, etc. And keep it. It is the best handbook for next year's camp, or to pass on information to those who come after.

A fresh approach to each camp. It is so easy to get into a 'we always do this' frame of mind. (Traditions the girls like to keep up are quite different.)

Enough rest, despite many last minute jobs, achieved by the gentle art of delegation. If to delegate wisely is going to help someone else, Guider or Guide, to progress, the Guider in charge is fulfilling her real function by creating the opportunity. This is sometimes the hardest thing for a good organiser to do!

A firm conviction that you will see your reward in the eyes of the girls, in the many achievements on their part, in the realisation that here more than anywhere else both you and your Unit are having the opportunity to live the Guide Promise.

Chapter 4.

ALL ABOUT TENTS

Whether your tent is the more solid 'dormitory' for your week's camp or the light shelter which accompanies your adventurous feet, it must be entirely reliable—waterproof and suitable for the weather conditions you might reasonably expect.

Choice of Tents

For standing camps it is preferable to have heavier tents—274, 342 or 411 gsm. cotton duck. The larger lightweight tents do not stand up so well in high winds and their life-span is much shorter. On the other hand they are cheaper and more versatile, as they can be used for camps where weight is a problem.

Ridge tents are generally more popular than bell tents, as they are easier for Guides to handle, being lighter, and easier to pitch and air. Many Companies, of course, may already own bell tents, which, because of their durability, will take a long time to wear out, so instructions for handling bell tents are included in this chapter.

For a Patrol of six a ridge tent of approximately 3·5 m. by 2·5 m. is required, while two Guiders will require a minimum of approximately 2 m. by 1·8 m., both 1·8 m. to 2 m. high for comfort. A large variety of suitable tents in these sizes and various sizes in between is available. Tents with a bell-end give very useful added luggage space. Tents which are 3·5 m. to 4 m. long frequently have a centre pole which, as well as relieving the strain on the ridge pole, provides useful hanging facilities for clothes, etc., clear of the canvas.

Tents with sewn-in groundsheets are unsuitable for standing camps as they cannot be aired and the ground will be badly marked when the tents are struck.

Tent Requirements for a Guide Standing Camp

One sleeping tent per Patrol (a ridge approx. 3·5 m. by 2·5 m. and 2 m. high or a bell). Tents for camp staff, according to number. (If camp beds are used fewer Guiders can be accommodated in each tent.)

One tent for central stores: a ridge tent which opens at both ends is best for this, as it is most easily aired, and one with high walls and standing room is preferable for comfort. For Patrol camping the store tent need not be large, as each Patrol will have facilities for storing food (see Chapter 5).

An extra tent, which can be used as a sick tent if required, is recommended, but in a very small camp, in an emergency, it may be possible to use a Guider's tent for this.

A marquee may be found useful, especially in a bigger camp, so that everyone can get together in wet weather, but when Guides are eating in Patrols there is not the same necessity to have one. Guides should never sleep in a marquee. They are rather vulnerable in a high wind and a falling pole might cause injury. More details about marquees are given later.

Details about toilet and wash tent requirements are given in Chapter 6.

Lightweight Tents

Rangers may well use lightweight tents in a standing camp, partly because they are easier to transport, and partly because, by owning such tents rather than heavy ones, they will have far more camping scope, using them also for mobile camps of various kinds. The smaller lightweight tents are very popular, as they stand much better in the wind than higher ones. Also they can be carried strapped to rucksacks. Two principal types of small lightweight tent are available—the two-pole 'bivvy'-type tent, with a maximum height of about 1·4 m., or a single pole tent with a maximum height of about 1·5 m. There is a wide range of such tents, some to suit every pocket.

Generally these tents will sleep no more than two comfortably, though with the single pole style tent it is sometimes possible to replace the pole with outside angle poles and accommodate more.

Lightweight tents with sewn-in groundsheets are useful for touring camps or camps of shorter duration but should be avoided for longer camps, as the ground will suffer.

Living in a bivvy tent for more than a week-end is not to be recommended for new and doubtful campers, especially in wet weather, when the canvas is liable to leak if touched. A flysheet (which is an extra roof stretched over the tent) solves this problem and also gives added protection, as with lightweight tents you can get a fine spray coming through when the rain is heavy. The eaves of the flysheet are also useful for storing stove, cooking utensils, etc. Disadvantages are, of course, extra weight and expense.

The tent requirements for lightweight camps will depend on circumstances and each case will have to be assessed on its merits.

The Different Parts of a Tent

The names of the different parts of a tent can be seen in the accompanying diagram (Fig. 7).

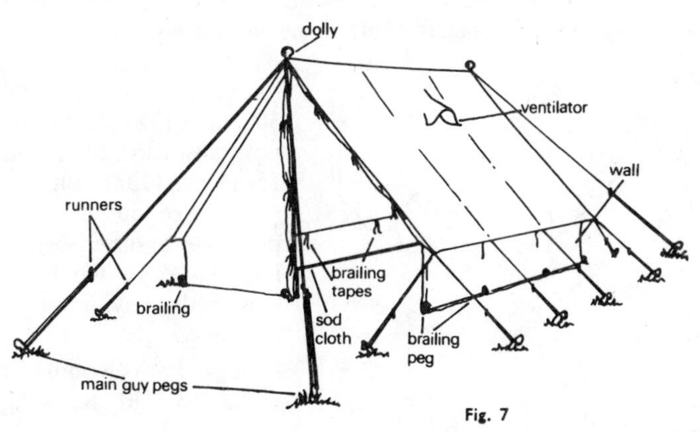

Fig. 7

All campers should become familiar with these names before going to camp—for obvious reasons!

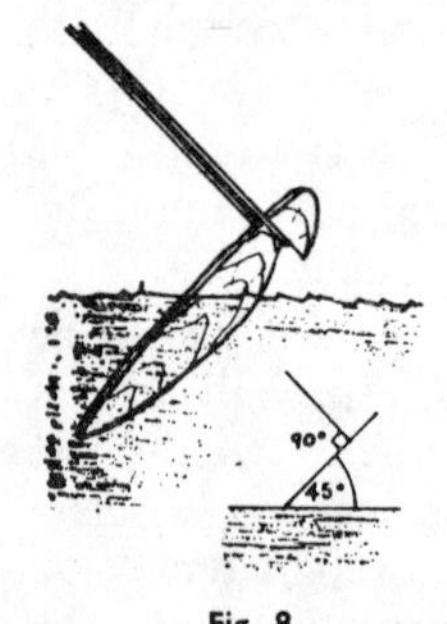

Fig. 8

Pegs. For heavier tents these are usually of wood, 40 cm. long for main guylines, 30 cm. for other guys, and 23 cm. for brailing. Longer pegs may be necessary in exposed sites with sandy soil. Wooden mallets are required to hit pegs into the ground.

To put in a wooden peg, stand behind it, holding it sloping slightly away from you. Give it a few taps to fix it in position. Then hit it hard with a good swing of the mallet, held in one hand only, until the notch is just far enough above the ground to hold the guyline clear of the ground (see Fig. 8). Pegs are removed by hitting them alternately back and front (not from side to side, which might split the peg) until they are loose enough to pull out. Finally, remove traces of the hole with mallet or heel. Have some pegs and mallets available for Patrols to practise this before going to camp.

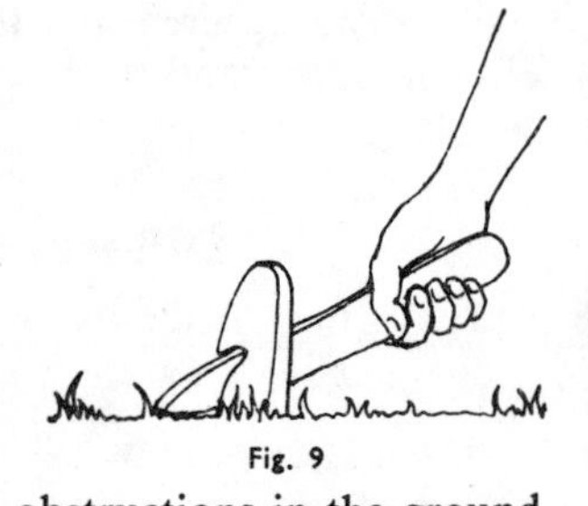
Fig. 9

Metal pegs are most usually found with lightweight tents. They can be put in by hand or with a rubber mallet. Care must be taken to avoid obstructions in the ground, as trying to force a peg in against one will simply bend it. For this reason it is not a good idea to use a wooden mallet. 30 cm. or 23 cm. pegs are normally used for guylines, 15 cm. ones for brailing.

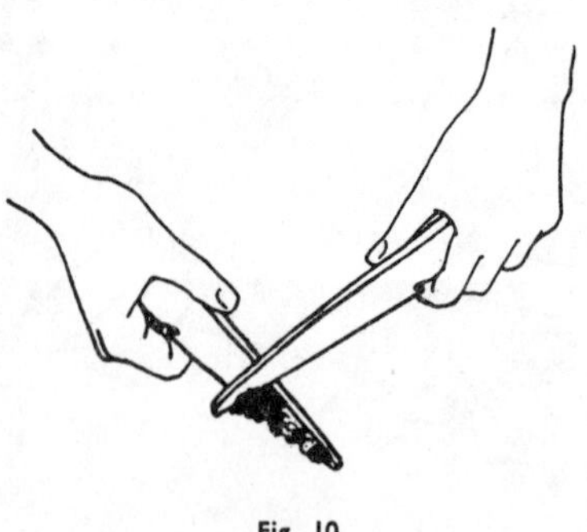
Fig. 10

To take out a stubborn peg, use another peg as a lever (Fig. 9). Do not pull it with the guyline or brailing loop.

Pegs, both wooden and metal, should be scraped

clean of earth and dried before being put away (Fig. 10). They should have their own bag and are normally packed in the tent bag.

Always take some spare pegs to camp to replace broken or lost ones.

Mallets. Wooden mallets are required to put in wooden pegs. A mallet is generally supplied with each tent, but it is useful to have a few extra, otherwise tent pitching is delayed. Mallets should be inspected before use for 'flying head' disease, which could have uncomfortable consequences for any victim in line! A loose mallet head can be tightened by soaking in water.

Poles. These are generally jointed and made of wood with metal joints, or of aluminium alloy. Ridge tents, except for the smaller lightweight ones, generally have two uprights (or three with the longer ones) and a ridge pole. Fitting the poles of unfamiliar tents together can be tricky, so it is worth marking them in some way, e.g., coloured rings with a different colour to each joint. It is also worth devising a system of knowing which set of poles belongs to which lot of canvas. To find yourself 50 miles from home with the wrong set of poles could put a serious strain on the seventh Guide Law.

Nothing should ever be hung from the ridge pole or from the cross bar at the apex of a frame tent (for which a suitable hanger is obtainable). Nails should never be driven into tent poles.

If you should be unlucky and find yourself in pole-trouble the following hints may be useful.

Poles too short: set on bricks. Poles too long: bury required amount. No ridge pole: pitch without, or use a rope. Fireshelter or screening poles can be used for tents and something improvised to replace them. It may never happen!

With frame tents it is wise to mark the pieces so that, if the spring comes out, there will not be undue difficulty in putting it together. (Replacement springs are obtainable.)

Wooden poles sometimes refuse to come apart after camp if the wood has swollen in the damp. If the strongest campers fail in a combination of twist and tug-of-war, try a *gentle* tap with a mallet on the metal joint, but do not persist if unsuccessful. Heat applied to the metal joint (causing it to expand) should do the trick and this works too with alloy poles.

Poles which do not fit into the tent bag should be very firmly tied, for transport, top and bottom. Using cord or thin rope (old nylon stockings are also very good), lay it in a figure S, lay bundle of poles on top, put an end through each loop, and tie ends securely (Fig. 11a and b). Big bundles of poles can also be secured with thick rubber bands cut from car tyre inner tubes. For rail travel it is wise to secure poles in hessian or old sacks before tying, as even the most securely tied bundles loosen with handling. It will not be funny if half an upright misses a connection through being separated from the rest of the party!

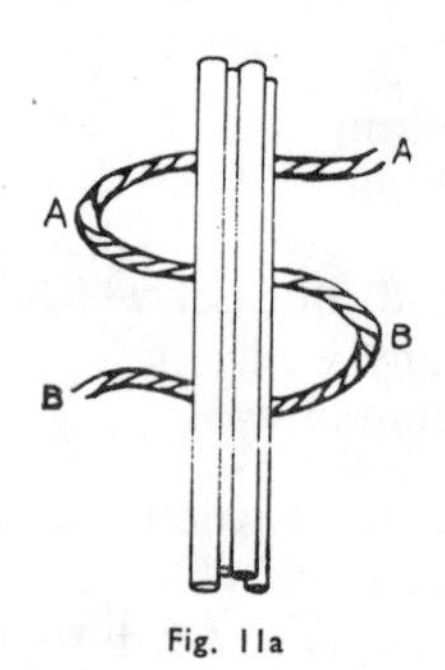

Fig. 11a

Canvas. The canvas is perhaps the most precious part of the tent and should be treated with the utmost care: not walked upon when pitching; no pins stuck into it; not put away unless absolutely dry (guylines and brailing loops as well), otherwise it will become mildewed and will rot. Care should be taken when folding or rolling a tent to see that no foreign matter that is likely to rot it is adhering to it.

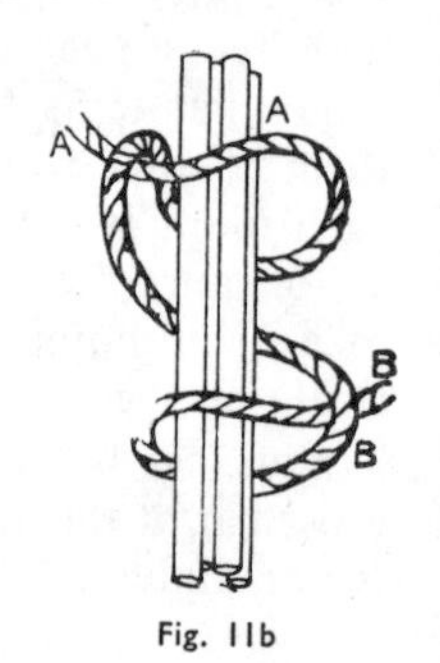

Fig. 11b

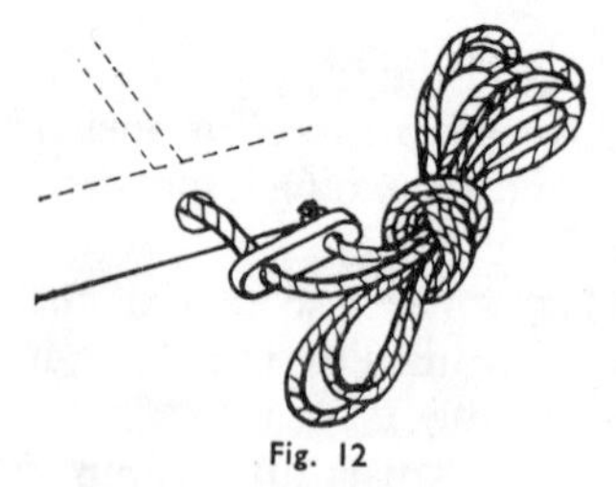
Fig. 12

Guylines. Guylines may be of cord or nylon. Nylon is useful because it does not shrink in rain but care must be taken to choose a runner which does not slip on it. Guylines should always be tied up before striking otherwise they become hopelessly entangled (Fig. 12).

Placing Tents

Tents should not be pitched too close together. If space is limited there should at least be room for two people to walk between the pegs. Patrols and Ranger groups generally like to choose their own private spots and such preferences should take priority over a uniform arrangement of tents.

Ground should be as level as possible, stones, thistles, and evidence of livestock removed, and any minor bumps flattened with a mallet. If there are rushes, go elsewhere. A spot with a dip in it, or even a slight track running through, is suspect as that is the sort of channel much favoured by rain-water.

Shelter is important but, despite the attractiveness, tents should not be pitched under trees, except perhaps for the store tent, for which shade is important. Elm trees are particularly fond of dropping a casual branch on the unwary.

Pitching Tents

The aim is to get the tent up, with poles and guylines straight and pegs in correct position, in a reasonable time, and any method that achieves this end is 'correct'. The best way to learn is to watch and help someone who knows how. The following suggestions are for those who have had little or no opportunity to obtain first hand experience.

The most efficient way is for someone to take charge and allocate the various jobs. With Guides this will be the P.L., or someone appointed by her, with others probably the most experienced member of the group.

To Pitch a Ridge Tent

1. Fit the poles together and lay out with the bottom of the uprights where you want them to be. Put in a peg to mark the bottom of each upright.

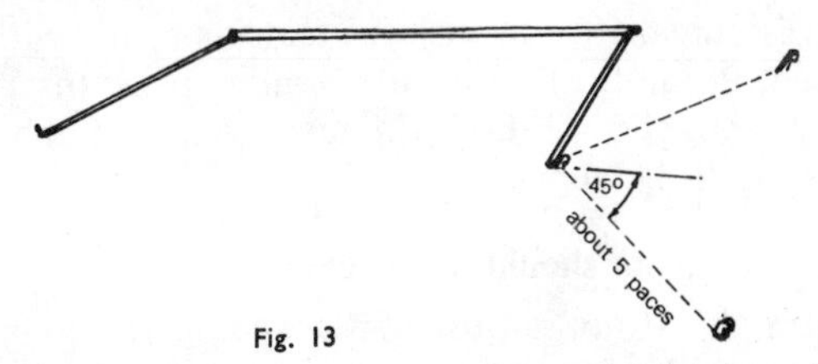

Fig. 13

2. Take the four largest pegs, two for each end, and put in at an angle of 45 degrees about five paces out (this distance may vary according to length of main guys) (Fig. 13).

3. Meanwhile others are rolling out the canvas ready to slip over the poles, looking out and untying the main guys, and making sure that the ventilators, if any, are open.
4. If there are loops inside the ridge of the tent, take off the ridge pole, slip it through the loops and replace it on the uprights. If there are no loops simply slip the canvas over the poles putting the spikes of the uprights through the holes in the canvas. Put the dollies with the main guys over the spikes.

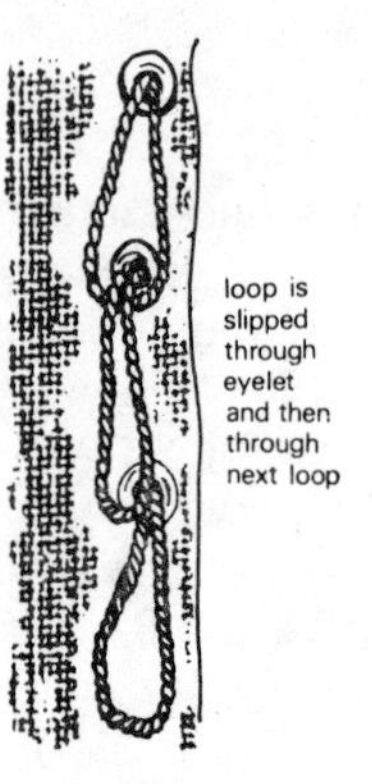

Fig. 14

5. Raise both uprights together and hold straight until the main guys are put on to the four pegs and tightened. The tent should now stand by itself.
6. Make sure the doors are closed (Fig. 14).
7. Put in the four corner brailing pegs. Meantime others can be untying the guy-lines and putting a peg ready for each.
8. Put in pegs for the corner guys. If there are two at each corner they go at right angles to each other, if one it goes at an angle of 45 degrees.

   NOTE: Pegs are placed so that the runner, when the guyline is tight, is one-third of the way up from the peg.
9. Put in the other pegs so that the guylines are straight.
10. Put in the rest of the brailing pegs, keeping the wall straight.

    NOTE: For a tent with no ridge pole, start by laying the canvas out where you wish the tent to be, and with the doors closed. Put in the four corner brailing pegs. Insert the poles. Hold straight until the main guys are secure and proceed as for other ridge tents.

The following points should be checked:

Poles straight. If not, adjust by slackening and tightening guy-lines, not by shifting the pole.

Pegs in a line, inserted at the correct angle, with the notch just far enough up to keep the rope off the ground.

Guylines in a straight line with the seam in the canvas, otherwise they put an uneven strain on the canvas, which in time will weaken it.

Runners facing the same way, for ease when slackening and tightening.

Storm setting. Tents with a ridge pole may be *storm set* (Fig. 15). This helps to hold the ridge pole firm in windy weather and gives more space in front of the tent. Care must be taken to see that the main guys do not touch the canvas, each other, or any of the side guys.

When working with familiar tents, it is possible to evolve your own way of pitching tents so that they are storm set right away.

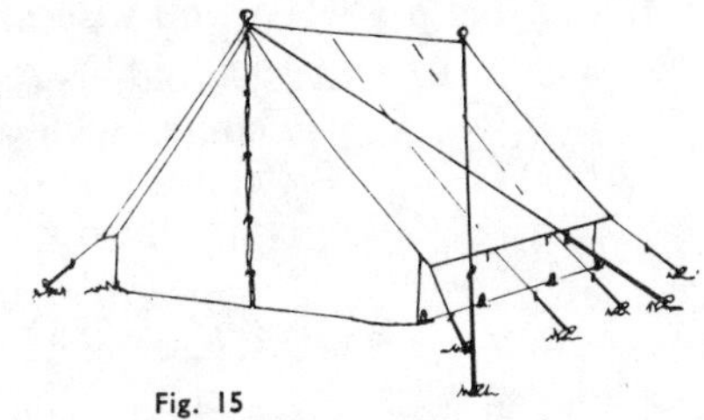

Fig. 15

To Strike a Ridge Tent

1. Take out brailing pegs, scrape and stack in a cobhouse (Fig. 16). Fasten doors.
2. Take out all pegs except those of the main guys, scrape and stack.
3. Roll up guys.
4. With one person holding each upright, remove main guylines and take out pegs.
5. Lower poles together into the wind.
6. Remove poles.

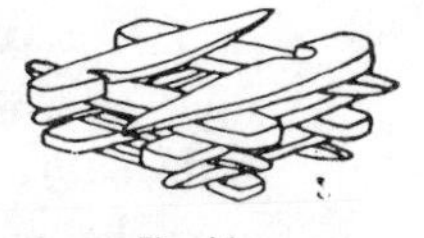

Fig. 16

   (Do the following as quickly as possible if grass is damp):
7. Pull canvas straight and remove grass, etc.
8. Fold in doors.
9. Fold canvas into centre or in three, the number of folds depending on the size of the tent bag.
10. Roll the folded canvas, starting at the ridge end, pushing out the air.

11. Pack the canvas immediately, along with the main guys.
12. Check the ground for missed pegs, peg holes, and litter.
13. When pegs are dry, pack in their bag. Put into tent bag with mallet. Insert the poles or tie up separately (as described on p. 38).
14. Fasten tent bag and label if necessary, e.g., if wet, in need of repair, or short of pegs.

To Pitch a Bell Tent

1. Put in a peg where you wish the bottom of the pole to be.

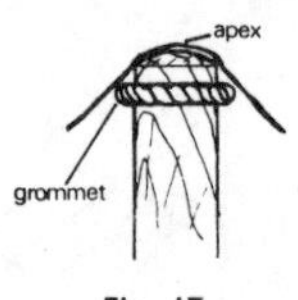

Fig. 17

2. Unfold the canvas and open out into a circle, with the grommet over the peg and the walls turned under, making sure that the door is closed.
3. Unroll the guylines in a straight line with the seams in the canvas.
4. Put in pegs for the four main guys. These are sometimes marked with different coloured runners. If not, take one at the door, one at the back, and one at each side. The pegs are put in two-thirds of the way down from the canvas.
5. A strong member of the team takes the pole, crawls in with it, inserts the top in the grommet (Fig. 17) and, with generally a little initial help from outside, raises it until the bottom touches the peg inserted at the beginning. Then she holds it straight until the main guys are tightened.
6. Other pegs are put in two-thirds of the way down the guylines which should be in a direct line with the seams in the canvas.
7. Put in the brailing pegs.

Points to remember:

Pole straight. Adjust by slackening and tightening guys, not by moving the pole.

Guylines in a straight line with the seam in the canvas. This is known as 'starring' the tent.

Pegs inserted at the correct angle with the notch just far enough up to keep the rope off the ground.

Runners facing the same way, for ease when slackening and tightening. You will quickly cultivate an eye for a bell tent and can tell at a distance whether it is well pitched.

To Strike a Bell Tent

1. Take out brailing pegs. Scrape, and stack in a cobhouse to dry.
2. Take off all but four main guys, tie up. Take out pegs. Scrape and stack.
3. With one person holding the pole, take off the four main guys and tie up. Take out pegs.
4. With one person at each side pulling the canvas out, lower pole gently.
5. Remove pole and straighten out canvas, removing grass, etc., turn in walls.
6. Fold canvas. There are various ways of doing this according to the shape of the tent bag. One way is to fold the apex down to the top of the door, fold into the centre twice, then one half over the other. Roll, pushing out the air as you do so. Put canvas in bag.
7. Check the ground for missed pegs, peg holes, and litter.
8. When pegs are dry pack in their bag. Put into tent bag with mallet.
9. Label tent if necessary, i.e., if wet, requiring repair, or short of pegs.

To Pitch a One-Pole Lightweight Tent

1. Spread out opened-out canvas with the door closed.
2. Put in the corner brailing pegs.
3. Insert the pole and raise until it is straight.
4. Put in front and back guylines first, then the other guys and brailing pegs.

To Strike a One-Pole Lightweight Tent

Remove pegs, tie up guylines, remove pole, and fold to fit bag. Clean pegs. Pack.

Flysheets

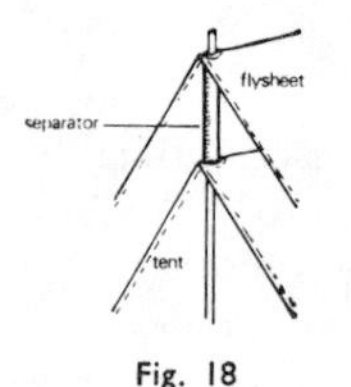

Fig. 18

A flysheet should be placed over the tent before the poles are raised. Generally there is a separator (Fig. 18) which fits into the top of the spike of the upright and leaves a gap between the tent and the flysheet. It is pegged out in the same way as the tent.

To Pitch a Frame Tent

The main operation is to fit the frame together, and it helps if you have seen the tent erected before attempting this yourself. If there are instructions supplied with the tent, follow these exactly and do not be tempted to take short cuts.

1. Sort out the uprights (which usually have solid ends or feet) and assemble the roof section at ground level. Move this to where you wish the tent to be and place the uprights ready for connection.
2. Place the canvas over the frame, and tie on in two places if the weather is at all windy.
3. Lift the frame, one side at a time if you are shorthanded, and insert the uprights. It is possible to do this singlehanded, but preferable to do all four corners at once to avoid straining the roof section.
4. Tie the canvas to the frame with the ties provided inside, and fasten the door(s).
5. Check that the canvas is accurately in place over the frame, then peg out the guylines and peg down the walls.

When pitching or striking in gusty weather it is easy to strain the frame if the wind is allowed to take control.

To Strike a Frame Tent

Simply reverse the process. Fold and pack as for an ordinary ridge tent.

NOTE: When assisting with pitching and striking a tent, get into the habit of looking to see what can be done next to save time, always treating main guys with healthy respect. Their untimely removal could prove unpopular with the rest of the striking party.

Marquees

Marquees can often be more bother than they are worth, especially on an exposed site, and with Patrol camping they are not required for meals. However, if the camp activities require numbers to get together frequently it is a help to have one in case of bad weather and especially if no solid shelter is near at hand.

Size of marquee required

For 30 campers approximately 6 m. by 3·5 m. or 4·5 m. by 4·5 m.

For 45 campers approximately 9 m. by 5 m.

Marquees may be square with one centre pole or oblong with two uprights and a ridge between. The canvas consists usually of a roof and separate walls which are hooked on all round. The poles are heavy and should not be dropped indiscriminately. Generally the help of able-bodied men is required to pitch a marquee that is much bigger than those mentioned above.

To Pitch a Marquee

One pole style

1. Drive in three or four stout pegs in a semi-circle where the base of the pole will be. Lay the pole with the base resting against the pegs. This will keep the pole from slipping when it is being raised (Fig. 19).
2. Put the roof over the pole and the dolly with the main guys on top.

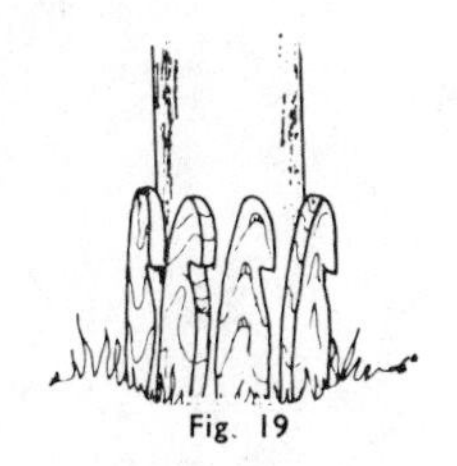

Fig. 19

3. Unroll the main guys (usually three). Pace out in three directions a distance of roughly half the width of the marquee plus 3 m. from the bottom of the pole and put in the three biggest pegs. (This distance may have to be adjusted, depending on the length of the guys.) Allocate one person to each guyline.
4. Two people raise the pole, assisted by the guyline holder on the appropriate side who pulls the rope.
5. Attach the guylines to the pegs with round turns and half hitches. The marquee should now stand.
6. Put in the four corner poles, pulling the roof as straight as possible, and peg out the corner guys.
7. Put in intermediate poles and guylines.

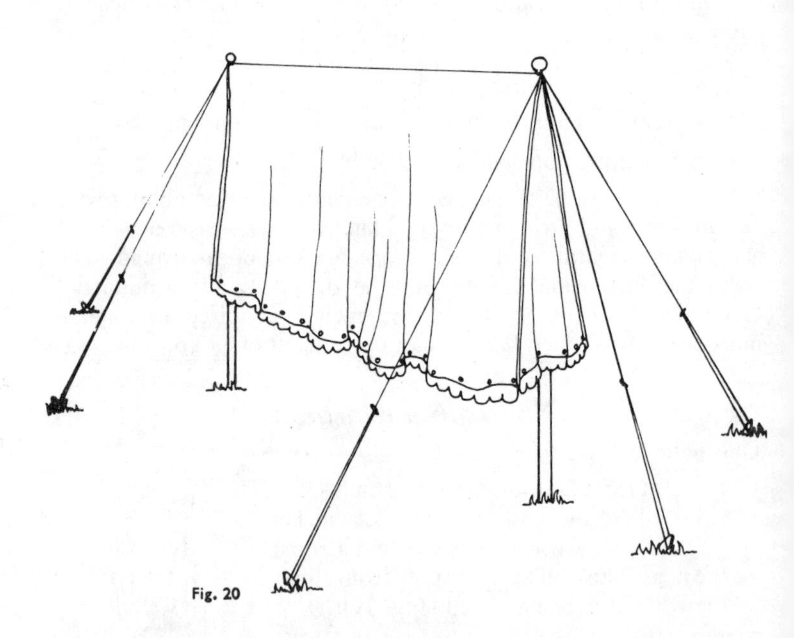

Fig. 20

8. Hook on the walls, outside the poles, making the join where you wish the door to be.
9. Put in the brailing pegs.

Two pole style

1. Fit the poles together, lay out where required, and unroll canvas roof.
2. Put in three or four pegs in a semi-circle at the base of each upright to anchor the pole when it is raised.
3. Insert poles in canvas as with a ridge tent, putting the dollies with the main guys on the spikes.
4. Put in the largest pegs for the main guys, three at each end. (Fig. 20). The distance of each from the base of the pole should be about half the width of the marquee plus 3 m.
5. With two people to each pole raise the poles together, with the help of those holding the guylines on the appropriate side.
6. Complete as for one pole marquee.

To Strike a Marquee

Reverse the process, remembering to put the semi-circle of pegs for the base of the pole before lowering it, otherwise the pole may slip or jump. Main guylines should be held and used to control the fall of the pole. Fold canvas, clean pegs and stack till dry.

Care of Tents

To avoid unnecessary wear and tear:

1. Guylines should be in a straight line with the seam in the canvas, and the poles straight. This ensures an even strain on the canvas. You quickly cultivate a tent 'eye' that spots if anything is wrong with the set of the tent.
2. Care must be taken that there is nothing rubbing against the canvas, particularly sharp points, or sticks. A gadget constructed when the guylines are tight may be quite clear of the canvas, but when guylines have to be slackened in rain or at night may touch or rub against the canvas. Kit should also be kept clear of canvas.

3. Guylines should not touch each other or the canvas, and should not touch the ground (except when the only way to keep the tent from blowing away is to drive the peg in far enough to anchor the rope).
4. A tent must never be packed away with any bit of it damp. Check especially sodcloth and brailing ropes. Damp causes mildew and the canvas rots. When a wet tent has to be packed temporarily, the bag should be so marked with the biggest possible label.

Care of Tents in Wet Weather

As rope shrinks when wet, guylines (unless nylon) sould be slackened in rain to allow for this, and also at night to allow for the effects of dew.

Care must be taken not to touch the canvas inside a tent, otherwise rain may come in. This is more likely in lightweight tents. Should it happen inadvertently, the worst can often be forestalled by drawing a finger down the canvas from the offending spot to the seam. Special care is needed to see that no kit is touching the roof when the guys are slackened, and that no clothes hanging from the pole are touching the tent door.

At night see that no corner of groundsheet is protruding from the tent. It could catch the rain, which would then run in on top of the groundsheet and soak someone's bed.

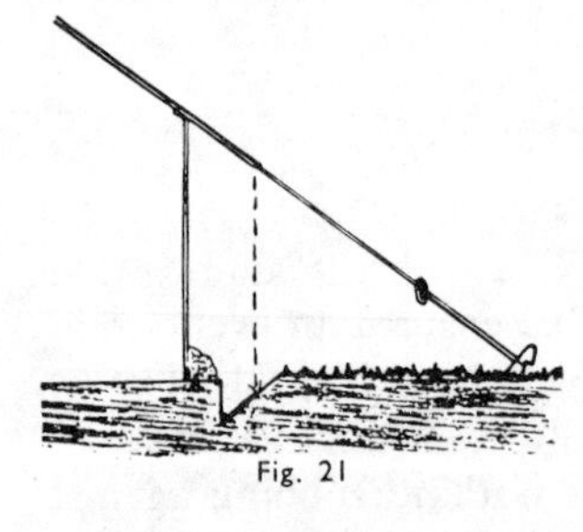
Fig. 21

In persistent wet weather, to prevent water running into a tent, a trench may be dug immediately under the eaves to catch the drips, the water being channelled away at the door. The turf should be carefully kept and replaced when the trench is no longer required. Note the angle of the sides of the trench. (Fig. 21)

Care of Tents in Windy Weather

Guys should be kept as tight as possible. If it is both wet and windy compromise by slackening the guys a very little at a time.

Keep the wind from getting into the tent (thereby lifting it and putting strain on guys and pegs) by keeping the door closed and the brailing tightly pegged down. If the brailing pegs are being whipped up, thread a rope through the loops and peg it down at the ends and at intervals with larger pegs (Fig. 22).

Fig. 22

Guylines slipping? Anchor them by twisting the rope round the runner (Fig. 23).

Fig. 23

Pegs jumping out? Use the longest available and hit in as far as possible. Devise any means available of anchoring the peg.

For example: Drive in another peg with its notch holding the first one down (Fig. 24).

Pile stones, bricks up against the pegs—anything to add weight (Fig. 25).

Put in two pegs in front, one at either side, with a rope attached to them and the first peg (Fig. 26).

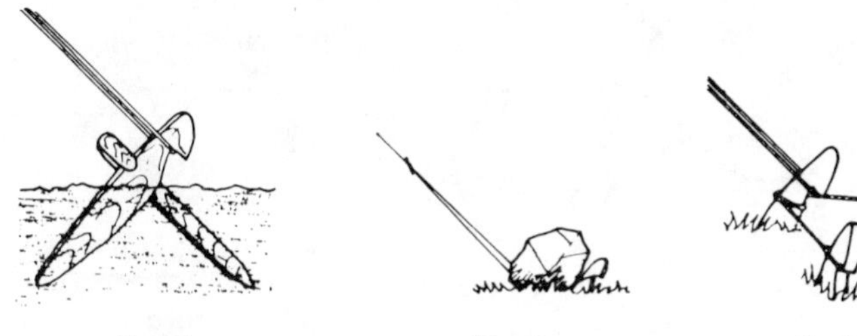

Fig. 24 Fig. 25 Fig. 26

Gadgets to assist pegs to stay in can be purchased. Keep your eye on catalogues. If rich, buy one, and try it out. If poor and/or proud, devise your own.

If all possible anchoring operations have been tried and the canvas threatens to tear (as may happen with a light or not-so-new tent), admit defeat, strike the tent and take to shelter. (Undamaged canvas is more valuable than undamaged pride.)

Marquees are particularly vulnerable in wind, and will probably require a dose of the above-mentioned peg-holding remedies. A regular watch should be kept on them in stormy weather.

Day to Day Care

In a standing camp tents should be aired daily. If the walls or sodcloth are damp loop the brailing to the outside (Fig. 27).

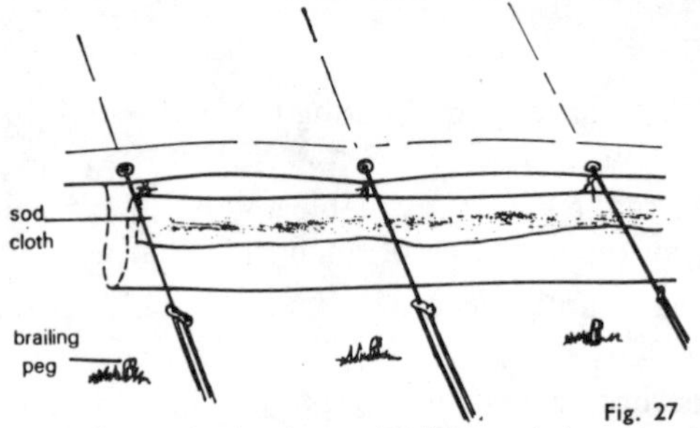

Fig. 27

When dry, roll up the brailing to the inside and attach by tying the tapes with the knot illustrated (Fig. 28), which is good for quick release, or if there is a loop inside, by putting the outside tape through the loop. If it is raining, tents can be aired for as long as is practicable by looping the brailing to the inside. This, along with checking for straight poles and guys, quickly becomes an automatic daily routine with the Guides.

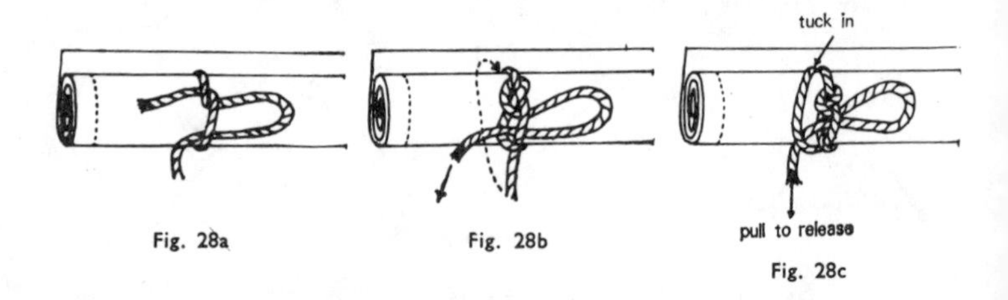

Fig. 28a Fig. 28b Fig. 28c

If a gale is blowing, however, the aim will be to keep the air out of the tent!

Marquee walls can be unhooked during the day in fine weather, leaving only the roof.

All kit should be off the ground during the day, the Guides improvising gadgets with wood, stones, or whatever is available on the site. (See Chapter 7). If stones are used they should be shifted daily, otherwise the ground will be marked. If the grass is not exposed to the air daily the ground will be badly marked, and the grass will rot and turn smelly. (Tents required for longer than ten days should normally be repitched on fresh ground.)

Nothing should be hung from the ridge pole. A stick, lashed to an upright (see Chapter 7) can be used for hanging clothes. With the frame tent nothing should be hung from any part of the frame. A special hanger is available which should be used only according to the instructions.

A far higher standard of tent care will be achieved from Guides who see it as a challenge to carry out the Guide Law and are trusted to do it, than any achieved because authority demands it, or resulting from a daily formal inspection at a certain hour. The Guider's role will be that of a watchful eye (especially with the less experienced) with encouragement and praise when due.

Repairs

Pegs. Spares should be brought. Broken pegs can sometimes be resharpened and used as brailing pegs, or retained to use as supports for boxes, etc. If you are stuck, a peg can be improvised from a green stick with a fork in it, or a notch cut out, and the end sharpened (Fig. 29). Butchers' skewers make substitute metal pegs.

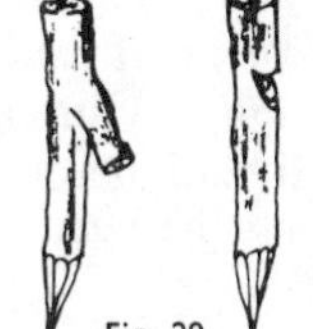

Fig. 29

Runners. If runners are missing and no spares are available, various slip knots can be used. One quick, effective way is to tie a clove-hitch with the 'loose' end round the guyline (Fig. 30);

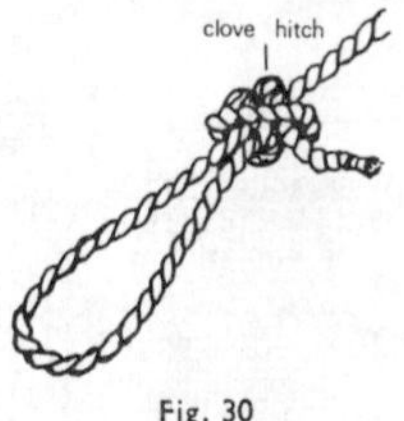

Fig. 30

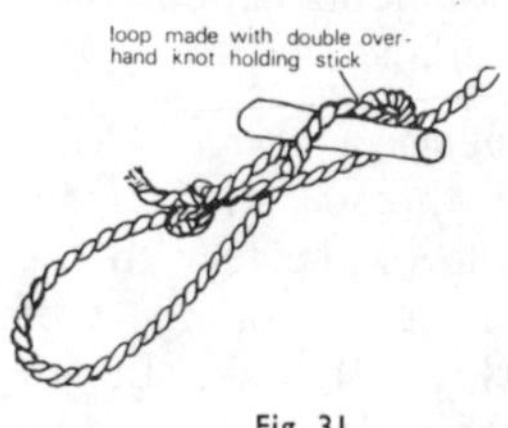

Fig. 31

another is to make a small loop at the end with a double over-hand, place it over the guyline, and push a short stick under the guyline—the stick acting as the runner (Fig. 31).

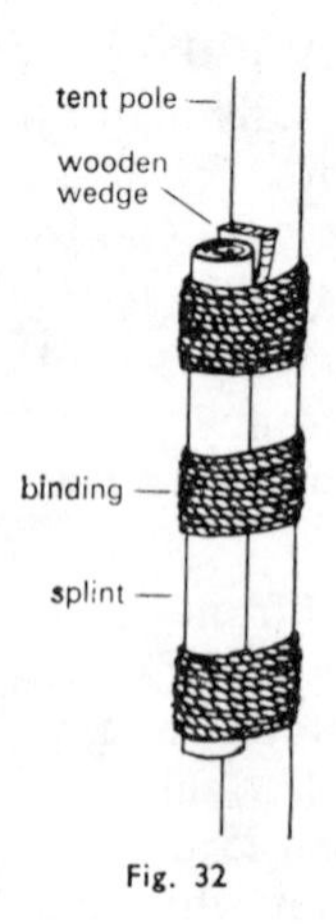

Fig. 32

Poles. A broken pole can be temporarily repaired by tying a splint to the pole where the break is, binding it at the top and at the bottom (Fig. 32). If further tightening is required, a wedge can be driven in between the splint and the pole.

Canvas. A small hole or tear can be temporarily repaired with a piece of adhesive plaster, or with warmed candle wax spread over with the finger. With a larger tear or hole a groundsheet with eyelets can be slung over the tent and pegged down by means of cords through the eyelets until a permanent repair can be made.

If the pole of a bell tent has gone through the grommet, put a small upturned pudding basin between the pole and the canvas.

Permanent Repairs

When sewing, to avoid leaving an unnecessarily big hole, use the smallest needle that will do the job. Flax or hemp thread suitable for the weight of canvas (look at the existing stitching) should be used. Use cobbler's wax to wax the thread before using. If you can get a sailmaker's palm for pushing the needle through it will make your task easier.

Patching. Use old or pre-shrunk canvas. (It is more easily cut with a sharp knife than scissors.) Apply on the inside wall, using a backstitch or improvised machine stitch. (Hemming is not suitable as it pulls the canvas.) Hammer the patch flat on a hard surface.

Mending a tear. Using waxed thread, stitch from one side of the tear to the other in a sort of figure of eight (Fig. 33). Make stitches of different lengths to distribute the strain of the canvas.

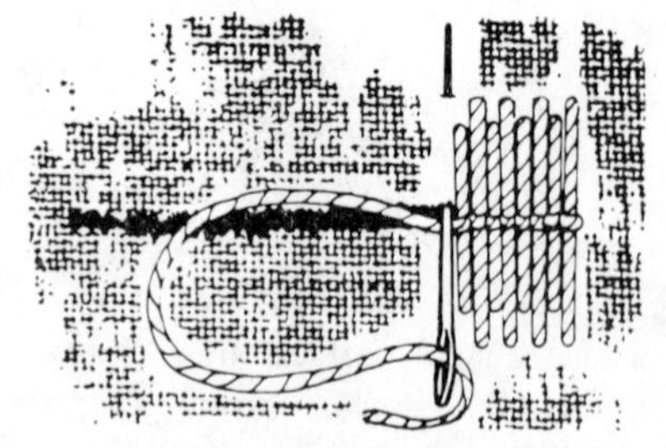
Fig. 33

Reproofing

All canvas can be reproofed and various preparations are obtainable. Make sure you obtain one suitable for the weight of the canvas, and before ordering work out the area to be covered so that you know the quantity that you require. Full instructions will be given on the container. Good heavyweight tents and the more expensive lightweight tents will (if well cared for) give many years' service before reproofing is necessary.

Storing

Tents must be thoroughly dry and free of decaying matter before being stored. They should be smoothly folded or rolled. Storage must be dry and both rat and mouseproof. Ideally tents should be raised off the ground to let air circulate below. Slatted shelves are good for this. Poles are best laid flat, but if they have to be stored upright, see that spikes are uppermost. Clearly labelled tents and poles give you a good start for your next camp!

Chapter 5.

FEEDING YOUR CAMP

A Guider running a camp will be expected to know how to cater for various sizes of groups under camp conditions. However, it is advisable, especially with a large camp, to have another member of staff detailed to act as Quartermaster—the traditional name for a camp cook/caterer.

General Arrangements

Feeding your camp sounds a vast undertaking but, in fact, it does not work out that way, because the Guides or Rangers feed themselves—one very important feature of our 'girl-run' camps. Being responsible for cooking their own meals gives the girls, apart from the more obvious 'skills' training, a feeling of confidence and a spirit of independence through a real sense of achievement. The team work behind it, the wood and water to be fetched, etc., gives an ideal and natural lesson in personal relationships—the Patrol System at work in a very real situation.

Patrol Camping

Patrol camping, in a standing camp, is therefore the logical arrangement to make to ensure most benefit to the girls, as far as meal preparation is concerned, and also the most fun. Cooking for five or six is much more like the real situation at home. Even the youngest can take a share in the actual cooking. 'Mum, I made breakfast twice for the whole Patrol', was how one eleven-year-old greeted her mother on her return from camp. Meals are prepared, cooked and served more quickly and food is hotter. Greater variety is also possible. Wood and water are generally fetched without too much prompting, as the girls realise only too well the effect of there being none! The Patrol Leader is responsible for delegating the various duties, but often it happens that the work just gets done because the need for it is immediately obvious. Guides used to Patrol camping, it has been found, are much readier to take the Patrol Camp Permit, and, on the whole, achieve a higher standard. The role of the Quartermaster in camp is to distribute the food. Generally, at the start of camp, Patrols are given a store of 'basics', the amount depending on the facilities they have for storing food. Q.M.s will probably find that a distribution once a day of other requirements will prove the most satisfactory arrangement and will discourage dropping-in visits for 'a loaf, please, Q.M., and some more jam'.

The other main functions of the Q.M. are to advise, when necessary, on how to cook certain dishes, and when to put things on, and to check on Patrol food storage and kitchen hygiene. The amount of advice given will depend on the experience of the girls.

Most Companies have the evening hot drink prepared centrally. Elevenses may also be served centrally and brings the whole Company together socially for a morning break.

Company Camping

If the cooking is done centrally, the role of the Q.M. is a much more arduous one, as the timing of meals for large numbers and coping with the large quantities is beyond the scope of all but the most experienced Guides, so considerable supervision by her will probably be required. Younger girls in the Patrol will have little opportunity for real cooking as pans are generally too heavy for them to handle. In Company camping Patrols generally take turns in doing the various chores involved in running the camp, so normally a different Patrol cooks each day.

Ranger Camps

Arrangements for cooking and catering will vary according to the programme, facilities for cooking, numbers, etc., and it is up to the Ranger Council to work out the solution for each case according to its merits. Sometimes they may wish to cook in small groups, but if numbers are small, cooking centrally for everyone may be the most practicable. This can be done by groups in turn or it may be that a small group will want to undertake the cooking for the duration of the camp.

Guiders' Camps

Cooking arrangements will depend entirely on the purpose of the camp. If there is a very full programme, it may be advisable to arrange for a group of Rangers, for example, to undertake the cooking. If the camp has a less demanding programme, Guiders will enjoy cooking in groups, with the informality and the opportunity for the much loved Guider 'brew-up' at any hour of the day or night! To base the arrangements and menu on what would be best for the Guide camp is neither necessary nor desirable.

Cooking Fires and Stoves

One of the thrills of camp is cooking on a wood fire, independent of gas and electricity. The fire seems to become the focal point of the camp, and the smell of wood smoke, brought home in camp jerseys or caught from a bonfire weeks later, brings back a rush of happy memories to the camper's mind. There is something missing from a camp with no fire.

However, wood fires generally require the presence of trees with accommodating owners, and sometimes this boon is denied the otherwise ideal site. Occasionally it is possible to arrange for a load of wood to be delivered, and this is often necessary for permanent sites where the local resources are exhausted before the end of the season. When camping on an island or by the shore you can often collect drift-wood, but make sure there is going to be enough, and remember that the supply can vary from year to year. The use of peat is another possibility but requires someone with experience in dealing with it, and bellows. A peat fire, however, has one great benefit: it can be kept in for the duration of the camp and simply brought to life with the bellows when required.

If all avenues of natural fuel have been explored without tangible result, or if it is simply a site where fires are not allowed, there is the possibility of using calor gas, butane gas, or primus stoves—a possibility certainly worth considering if the site has attractions which outweigh the unique attraction of a wood fire.

There are occasions, too, when a camp is held for a special purpose, and this may often be the case with Ranger camps, and more time can be devoted to programme if 'artificial' cooking arrangements are made. With mobile camps especially it is advisable to have stoves, unless you have ascertained that firelighting is permitted at all your stopping places.

Fires

It is essential that the ground is not damaged by your fire. If a bare patch is available in a suitable spot it can be used, particularly for one night or a week-end camp. (For a longer camp, you need to be sure that you will not be ankle-deep in mud if it rains.) Otherwise, there are two alternatives:

(i) **Turfing.** Dig out an oblong of turf, extending at least six inches beyond your fire all round (to keep the grass from catching fire). Sods should be stacked, watered daily, and replaced at the end of the camp.

(ii) **A raised fire.** This is recommended and often insisted on when a site is frequently used, and consists of a raised platform on which the fire is built. There are various ways of achieving this, depending on what is available, but the first essential is that it is absolutely secure and that there is no danger of pots toppling off the fire—for the safety of bystanders' legs even more than the contents of the pot! The supports of the fire can consist of piles of bricks at the centre and sides, milk crates, or big tins weighted with earth. (Wooden boxes are not suitable. They may burn unless protected with asbestos sheeting, and this is expensive, heavy, and easily broken.) A sheet of corrugated iron, with corners well turned under to prevent injury, is placed on top of the supports. On top of this is spread a layer, about three inches deep, of sand or earth, which will both level off the surface on which to

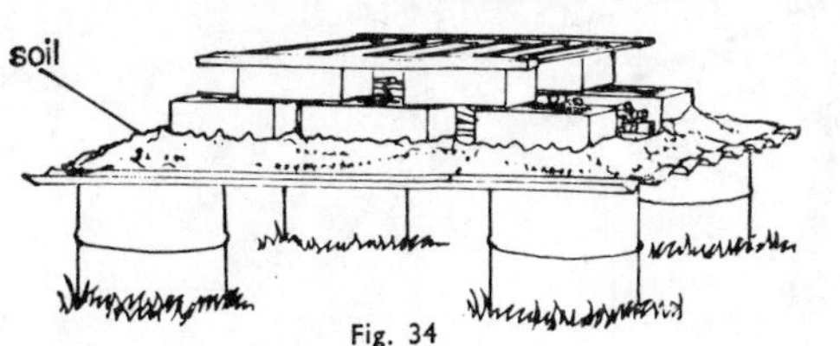

Fig. 34

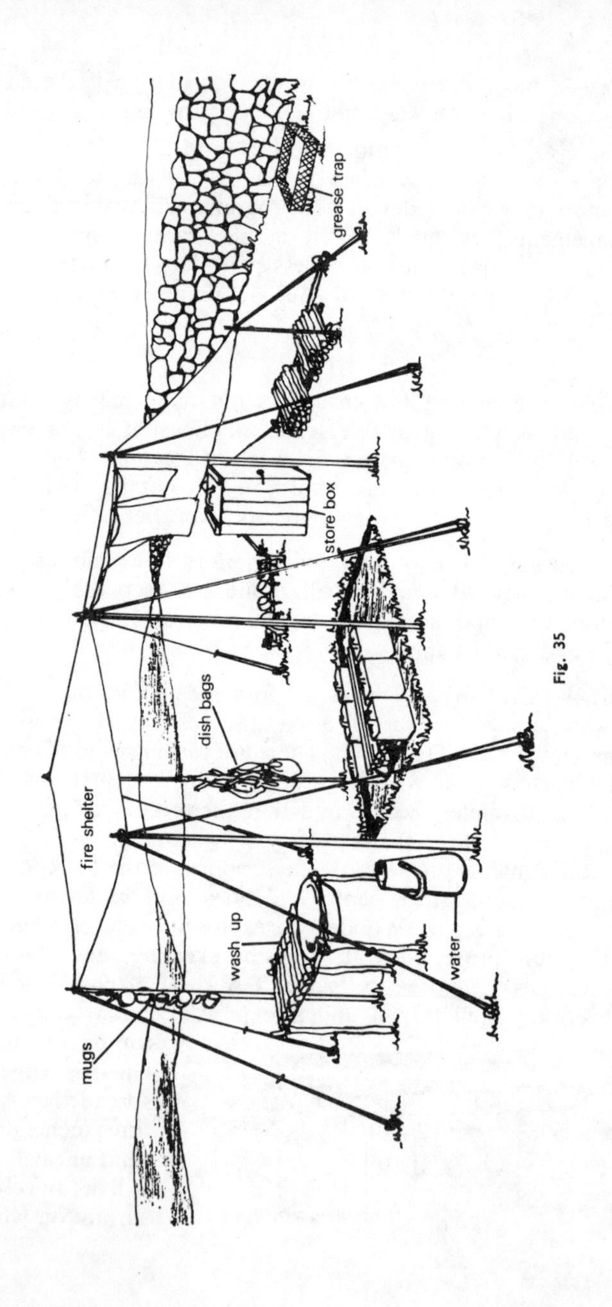
grease trap
store box
dish bags
fire shelter
wash up
water
mugs

Fig. 35

make the fire and prevent too much heat from going downwards (Fig. 34).

The actual fire. A favourite model consists of two rows of bricks, two deep and about 23 cm. apart with slight gaps between the bricks to let the air in, with a grid across the top on which to set the pans. A doorscraper makes a good grid, but a cheaper model can be achieved with the oven shelves and top bars of redundant gas cookers.

A modified version of the above, if the site is very exposed or the bricks are few, is obtained by digging a shallow trench (a spade's breadth wide)—T-shaped for the sake of draught, with the top of the T towards the prevailing wind and an extension at the other end to allow for stoking.

Where the supply or transport of bricks is a problem (as it can be when Patrol camping) it may be possible to get a firegrid constructed with legs and solid side pieces—the latter in sections so that some draught can get in. (If the fire has no sides the wood tends to fall out and blow away in windy weather.)

A crafty dual purpose fire, very suitable for Patrol camping, can be made with a firegrid on legs and 4 to 6 oblong 4–5 l. tins placed upright along the sides, half filled, at least, with water and the caps removed (this is important). This provides, as well as protection for the fire, an excellent supply of washing-up water (Fig. 36).

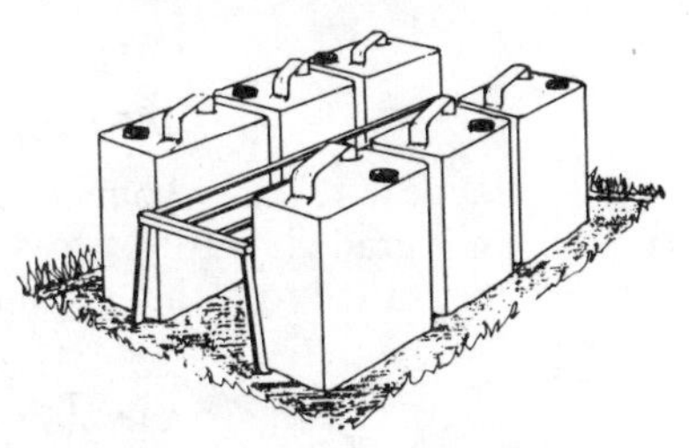

Fig. 36

If the firegrids can be made with legs sloping slightly outwards they will stack inside each other for easy transport and storage.

Fires for lightweight camps. Generally, unless transport is provided, Rangers will not want to carry bricks, grids, etc. If staying on the spot for a day or two, bricks may be borrowed locally or suitable stones found and placed close enough to let pots rest on top. Otherwise various types of hike fire or portable stoves can be used for cooking.

Firewood

If you tell your Guides which woods are best for burning they may not remember. But if you let them try them out they will not only remember, but learn which is which by sight, so wood recognition is a very worthwhile pre-camp activity. They will find out, for example, that fir and other resinous woods (except pine) burn well and brightly, with plenty of flame; that beech, birch, oak, and ash burn well but more slowly; and that chestnut, sycamore, and lime get progessively smokier, while elm and elder just do not co-operate at all.

For starting a fire fir is therefore good, as are birch and beech twigs, dead hawthorn, gorse, or holly. In camp the wise will also save butter wrappings, etc. (milk cartons make especially good firelighters) and ensure a supply of dry kindling for the morning.

After the fire is going, bigger sticks should be used, and Guides need a lot of convincing, too, that embers are hotter than flames, so that slow burning woods should be used, reserving kindling for lighting and reviving. In wet weather, wood can be dried off round the fire in advance, and alternated with wet for stoking.

Woodpile

It is practical to keep your wood supply, broken into handy lengths and graded, easily accessible. It should, for obvious reasons, be raised off the ground, this being achieved most simply by laying two logs about the length of the broken wood, one at either end of where you wish the woodpile to be, then lay three or four long branches across them at right angles to form a platform. The enterprising may wish to devise a more elaborate stand. Unless you have the type of fireshelter which takes the woodpile under its wing (q.v.), some sort of cover will be required to keep the wood dry. Old groundsheets usually spend their semi-retirement in this way. Unless the camp is of very short

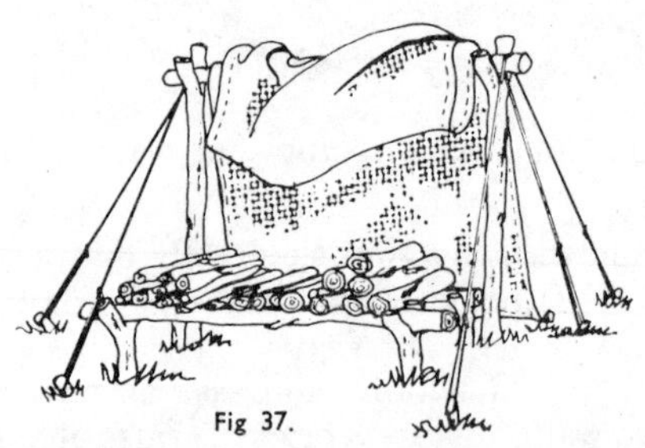
Fig 37.

duration it is worth devising some sort of framework over which to sling the cover, so that it forms a proper roof at night and in wet weather (Fig. 37). While aesthetically it may offend, it is wisest to have the kindling in the middle, as that is likely to be the best protected part of the woodpile.

Fireshelters

In our uncertain climate it is advisable to use fireshelters in standing camps. These can be bought, or made to suit needs and purses. If you are making your own, it is worth remembering that the wind can put a great strain on fireshelters, so canvas should be stout (at least 274 gsm. weight) and corners should be strongly reinforced.

The essential features of a fireshelter are that it should cover the cook as well as the fire and allow her to stand straight. Having to work in a permanent angle of 45 degrees is one of the less popular hazards of camp life.

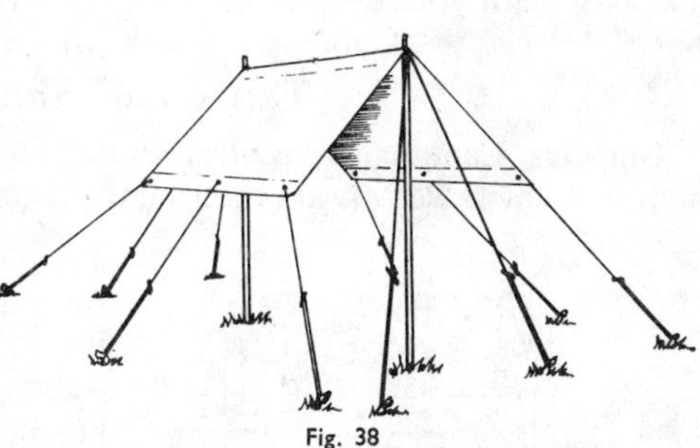
Fig. 38

If you study the accompanying diagrams you may find a fireshelter to suit you, or you may prefer to design your own model. (If you do not have facilities for sewing the canvas yourself, many firms will make it up to your specification.) Models range from the simple 'roof over a ridge' style to the superior 'Dutch style' fireshelter, which takes even the kitchen sink! (Figs. 35 and 39). The overall dimensions of the canvas are 2·25 m. by 6 m. As it takes woodpile and storebox as well, woodpile shelter and store shelter are dispensed with. A Company that camps a lot will find this type of

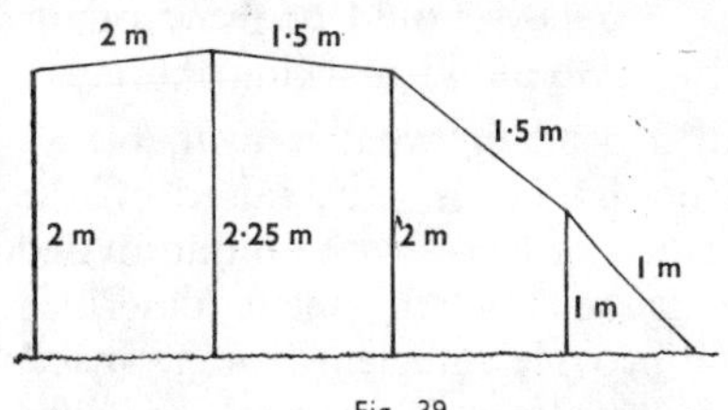

Fig. 39

kitchen with its many facilities well worth while. Guides find it much easier to keep everything tidy, and take great pride in their kitchens.

Stoves

If, for reasons mentioned already, stoves are to be used, there is a wide range available to suit need and purse: butane gas (widely popular so that refill cylinders are readily obtainable), calor gas (check on availability of refills if such is preferred), primus (rather trickier to use), etc. When using these out-of-doors it is advisable to rig up some sort of screen or shelter to protect them from the wind. Some of the smaller stoves, though light to carry, are less secure unless placed on very even ground. So if weight does not matter it may be wise to take some sort of flat base with you, e.g., an old tray.

Store Tents and Shelters

Standing Camps. A central store tent will generally be required unless Patrols are catering for themselves independently.

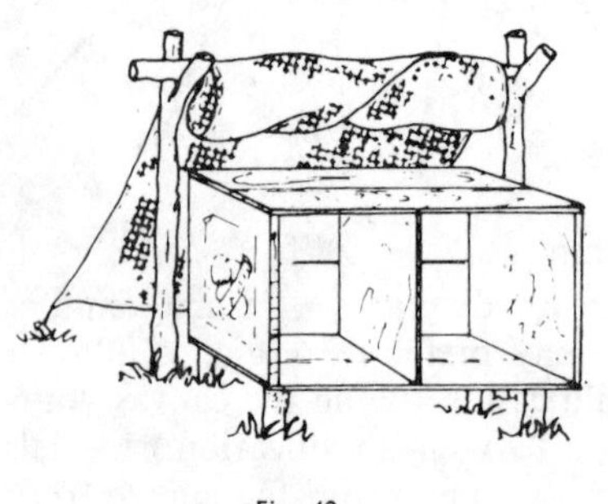

Fig. 40

This should preferably be a ridge tent with two doors, for airing, and with high walls, to allow height for boxes. Store boxes should be raised off the ground. (Old pegs can be kept for this, or short lengths of stout stick with pointed ends used.) If bricks or stones are used, they should be moved daily to avoid marking the grass.

Shelter for Patrol stores will depend on what is available. A bivvy tent may be used, with orange boxes, etc., raised off the ground as described above, or a box or boxes with an improvised shelter over them (Fig. 40). If using the Dutch fire-shelter described above, a store box (Fig. 41) will provide sufficient storage space. This box (approximately 100 cm. by 50 cm. by 50 cm.), provided with handles, can be used to carry the Patrol equipment to camp. It is then turned on end and two movable shelves inserted to make adequate cupboard accommodation for food and utensils, which will be readily at hand for the cook.

Lightweight Touring Camps. Rangers can have a lot of fun devising means of carrying and storing food, which will be both light for travelling, and weather and animal-proof for stops. Foil wrapping and plastic containers with sealing lids will no doubt top their list, as these have the additional benefit of prolonging the freshness of the food provided they are kept in the shade. They will also find thermos flasks handy. These solve, for example, the problem of transporting the half-used bottle of milk. For week-end camps light shelters may be devised on the principle of the Patrol shelter illustrated on p. 62. (See also notes on storing food on p. 78).

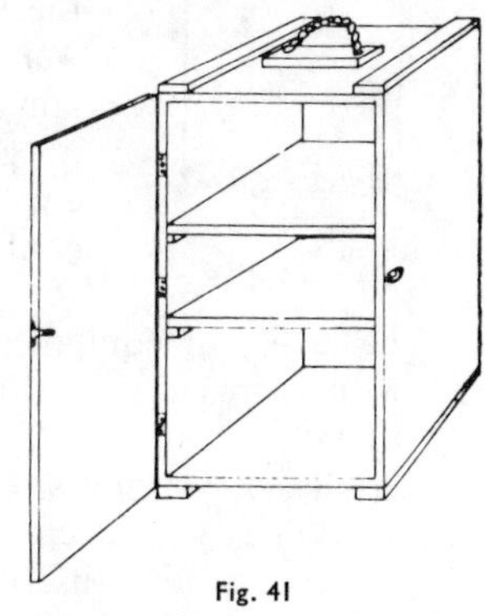

Fig. 41
Store box, 100cm × 50cm × 50cm deep

Cooking Utensils

Patrol Equipment

The Patrol will have great fun and a real sense of achievement if they build up their own set of equipment by making as much as possible and raising money for the rest. Until the equipment is complete many items can be borrowed from home, but Patrols will take tremendous pride in equipment that is *theirs* alone, and will make great efforts to keep it in good condition. In a Company, Patrols often choose their own camp colour, and try to buy or paint the items of equipment in that colour. As well as looking very attractive, this makes administration easier. (You will know immediately who left that dirty blue basin where it shouldn't be!).

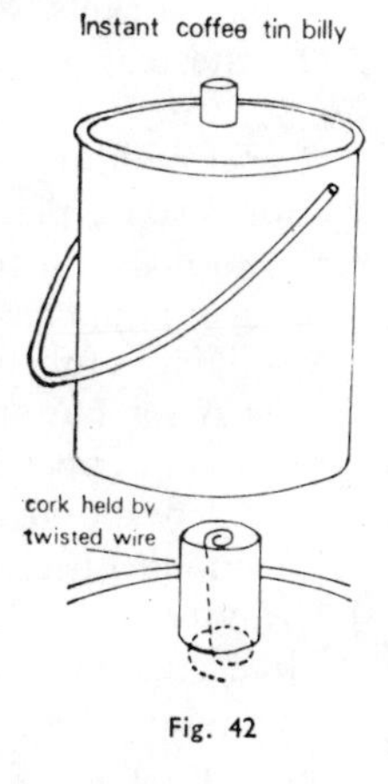

Fig. 42

Much can be gathered at no cost. Tins or screw top jars can be used for 'basics'—tea, sugar, flour, etc. With jars there is the danger of breaking in transit, but tins, unless they can be put away really dry and stored in a dry place, will rust. Empty coffee tins with wire handles attached to the lids make effective water boilers (Fig. 42), and these too, along with empty 3 kg. jam tins, can be used as Patrol refuse tins or grease traps (Fig. 43). Guides, with encouragement, will soon develop a 'what-could-we-use-that-for-in-camp' eye.

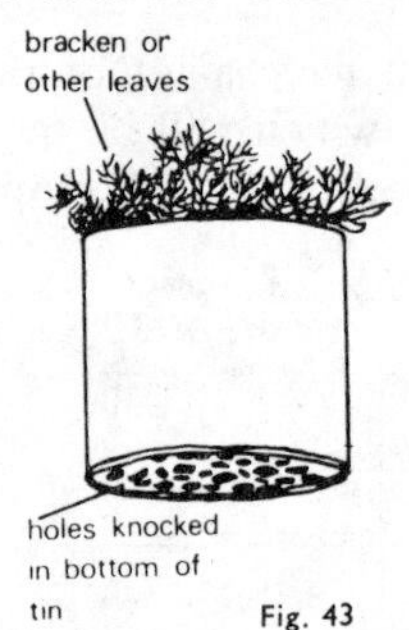

Fig. 43

A basic list of equipment, to which the Patrol may wish to add with increasing wealth or more ambitious culinary aims, might be:

3 pans of varying size (e.g. 1½ l., 1 l. and ½ l.). A nest of billies with deep lids which can be reversed for keeping things hot is useful.
1 frying pan.
1 kettle or water boiler for washing up water. This can be dispensed with if cans are used at the side of the fire. (See p. 58).
1 or 2 plastic bowls for washing up.
1 or 2 buckets.
1 water carrier with cap (4½–9 l.). This is kept for drinking water.
2 or 3 pudding basins.
2 or 3 spare plates, not all plastic. If used for keeping food hot over a pan, plastic would melt.
1 jug or liquid measure.
Containers for 'basics'—sugar, tea, etc.
Dishes for butter, sugar, jam.
Salt and pepper containers.
Wooden spoon, fish slice, ladle, serving spoon, tin opener, potato peeler, grater, spare cutlery.
Teapot.
Grease trap.
Camp larder.
Muslin covers, potholders, panscrubber, dishmops, etc.

Central Equipment

(when Patrol camping)

1 large pan or dixie (9 l. size will serve 30 for evening hot drink).
A large kettle is useful.
I small kettle or boiler.
Cooking utensils for staff, depending on what meals they will be cooking for themselves.
Jugs for serving hot drinks and elevenses.
Liquid measure.
3 or 4 serving trays.
Plates.
Spare cutlery, including a sharp knife, tin-opener, etc.
2 or 3 buckets.
2 or 3 bowls (for washing up, etc.).
2 gallon water carrier (for drinking water, etc.).
Camp larder.
Boxes and tins for store tent (boxes may be borrowed from grocer or greengrocer).
Selection of polythene bags.
Muslin covers, pan scrubber, dishmops, etc.

Company Camping

(The size of utensils required will depend on the size of the camp).

Requirements are as Central equipment above with a minimum of 4 large pans or dixies, plus:

1 large frying pan.
Urn for tea if numbers are more than 24.
Extra jugs.
At least 4 buckets and 2 water carriers.
1 wash-up basin per Patrol plus 1 or 2 extra.
Mixing bowls.
Selection of trays, etc.
Containers for butter, sugar, jam, salt, and pepper.
Implements as for Patrol camping (ladles, wooden spoons, etc.).

Lightweight Camps

Ingenuity is the first essential in any list!

For cooking pans probably one of the lightweight aluminium cooking sets will prove best. Study catalogues and choose the size which will cover the most possible occasions.

Where weight and bulk matter, canvas or oilskin buckets and basins can be bought (or made).

Plastic water carrier for drinking water. (You can get the kind that folds up when empty.)

These basic essentials can be added to, according to conditions, menu, or exchequer.

Half the fun of planning such a camp is working out what will be needed!

Note on Equipment

Polythene is light and wears well, provided it is not overheated so is not suitable for keeping things hot. It is more difficult to keep clean. Basins, bowls, and buckets in polythene are very suitable for camp, however, and their gay colours attractive. Choose buckets with metal handles for preference.

Enamel is quite good, and dishes withstand heat, but it is inclined to chip and should no longer be used for food when this happens.

Aluminium is more expensive but will last longer and is better, on the whole, than enamel for pans.

If buying new pans, make sure the handles are suitable for open fires, remembering they will get very hot.

Some Useful Kitchen Gadgets

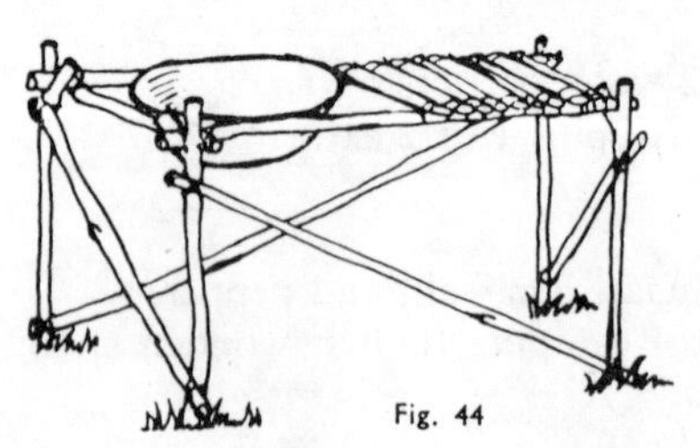

Fig. 44

Wash-up table. The time spent making this is well worth while. Washing up will be quicker and more hygienic and the kitchen will be permanently tidier (Fig. 44).

A pot rack is also useful and need not be elaborate (Fig. 45).

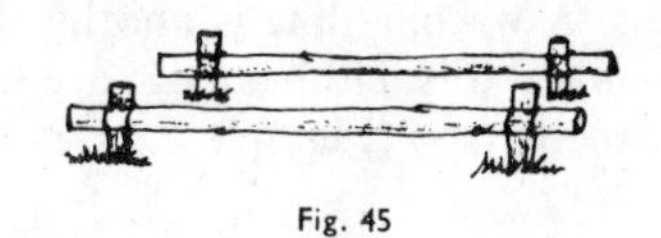
Fig. 45

Mugholders are handy. A mug tree can be constructed if an accommodating branch is available, or mugs can be hung on toggles from a strategic point (Fig. 46).

Fig. 46

Larders are essential. Even a very simple one is effective provided it is flyproof. (Clothes pegs can often be used to ensure this) (Figs. 47 and 48).

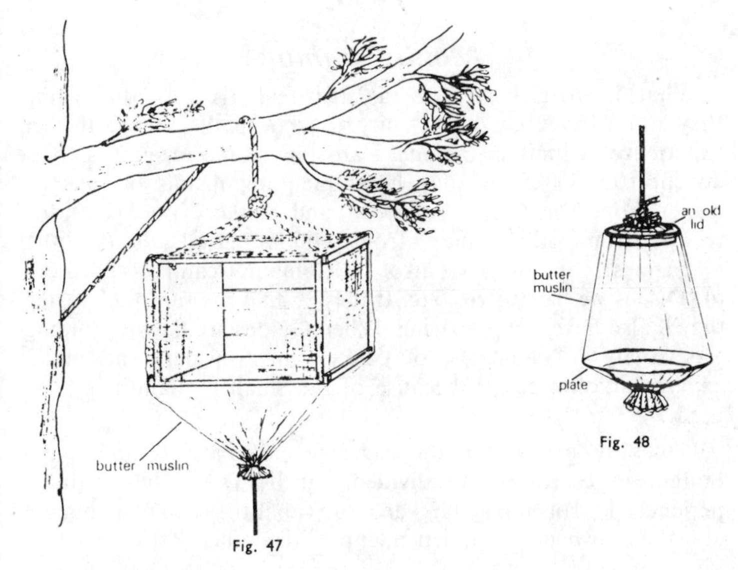

Fig. 47

Fig. 48

A washing line is another essential. If two ropes are twisted to make this, clothes pegs are not needed. (Corners are put through the twists) (Fig. 49).

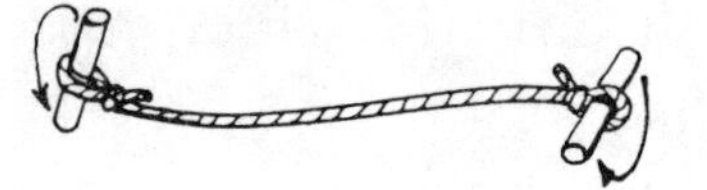

Fig. 49a
Rope twisted in opposite directions

Fig. 49b
Rope held at centre and allowed to twist

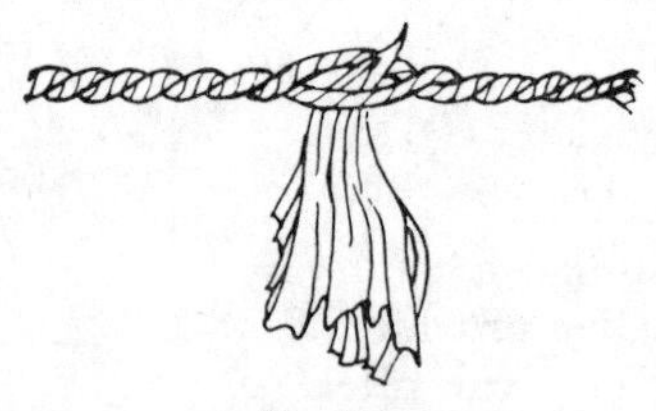

Fig. 49c
Washing held by corners without pegs

Food

Menu Planning

What do the girls want to eat? If it really is to be their camp, they must have the opportunity to choose the menu. If their experience is limited and ideas are few, some incentives to be adventurous in eating may help: planning menus or selecting dishes from *The Guide Handbook* and cookery books; finding recipes from other lands, from Guide periodicals or other magazines; compiling a Patrol or Company camp recipe book of 'Dishes we have tried', etc. If they've had the fun of choosing, they'll also have fun preparing. When Guides are Patrol camping, the variety of choice is, of course, much wider, and makes experimentation easier, because of the smaller quanitities being used.

Generally menus are the same for all Patrols, food being bought in centrally and divided out by Q.M., but with experienced Patrols it may be even more fun if they can plan, budget, etc. their own needs, independent of the other Patrols. A little (surreptitious) supervision of plans will probably be necessary! Less experienced Patrols may enjoy cooking one main meal during the camp with their own independent choice of menu, perhaps in the form of a cooking competition.

Rangers will probably want to undertake the catering themselves, the amount of supervision depending on the experience of those involved, but always reduced to the minimum.

However, when the Guides or Rangers are planning the menu, they may need a few hints about certain factors which must be taken into consideration.

1. To check that they have sufficient pots and 'fire-space' for what they plan to cook at a time. (It is no use planning soup, meat, two veg. and pud. if you have only three pots.) Rangers can have fun planning 'one pan cookery' if dependent on one portable stove.
2. To remember that you have no fridge in camp and menus may have to be geared to 'delivery day' or 'butcher's van day'. The secret is to start with the days when you expect to receive fresh meat, sausages, etc. and work from there. Guides find this sort of planning fascinating, like a jigsaw puzzle, but with a more satisfying end product! (And it is good training, too!).
3. The menus must be well-balanced, varied, and not include too many fries. They may know that a change of diet and air may cause constipation and will plan counter measures in the second and third day menus. Rangers and Guides have a wonderful opportunity of putting already acquired knowledge into practice.
4. While these practical and administrative points are essential, the first consideration in meal-planning *must* be the camp programme, and meals *must* be arranged to fit in with this and not vice versa. Meals that do not take too long to cook are generally best, unless, of course, cooking *is* the programme. With Patrol-sized groups, cooking need take no longer than at home. Larger numbers need a progressively earlier start. It is very disappointing to Guides if they have to leave an exciting ploy to put the potatoes on.

Sometimes, especially in Ranger camps, it is found to be best to plan a picnic-type lunch, which can be eaten anywhere to fit in with what is being done. Guides may wish to adopt this idea for every day, for some days, or for one day only.

Some Notes on Meals

Breakfast. Although many girls do not have a cooked breakfast at home, they welcome it at camp, where the fresh air and the exercise give them appetites. The 'body' acquired as a result of a protein breakfast may help to discourage over indulgence in starchy and sweet foods later in the day. When Patrol camping the staff usually prefer to make their own breakfast. It obviates possible delay for them and protects those with a slow-awakening social sense.

Elevenses. This is often served centrally. Squash and lemonade crystals are popular and can be served hot on a really cold day. Rangers may (or may not) have more sophisticated tastes.

Lunch and Evening Meal. The programme will determine which of these is to be the main meal and which the lesser one, and whether there will be tea in the afternoon. Guiders are usually invited to Patrols for main meals. This is an excellent training in hostessing for the Patrol or group and gives the Guider an opportunity to get to know the girls and vice versa. It usually develops into a very happy social occasion.

Late drink. This is often best prepared and served centrally. Cocoa may be the choice of the girls, but some Companies have more discriminating palates and like the choice of coffee or chocolate. This has an advantage in that any surplus milk or milk and water mixture can be used in a more versatile way than can cold cocoa.

Packed picnic meals. Some will favour sandwiches, but many prefer to dispense with the bulk or the superfluity of calories involved. Crispbread is sustaining and light to carry and potato crisps are also popular. Protein can be in the form of cubes or portions of cheese, hard-boiled eggs, cold cooked sausage etc., Dates and raisins are sustaining, perhaps with a biscuit and piece of chocolate. Tomatoes, apples, or some other fresh fruit complete the balance. Pack in polythene bags which can bring home the scraps.

For the last meal in camp, it is a good idea to pack a large polythene bag with a selection of the above for each Patrol or group. Then there is no washing up to do after utensils have been packed as no dishes are required and there are no unwanted curly sandwiches to lose after pig pails are emptied and pits filled in. Each Patrol can eat when it has finished its strike and the P.L. takes home the scraps in the bag!

Cooking Meals

In Patrols the P.L. usually works out a rota for cooking. probably two on duty at a time, so that all have a turn. If Company camping, Patrols take it in turn. In Ranger or Guiders' camps the arrangements are more flexible, with perhaps one member of each group assisting with each meal, or the same group undertaking to do all the cooking.

Q.M. directs operations as little as possible. Experience, however, will teach her that girls of Guide age are much slower, generally, than adults, and have to start preparations much sooner.

She will know the best kind of fire to use (see Fires on p. 57) and how not to singe the custard. She will know that a high wind can slow down cooking. She may also have to advise on how to keep things hot on plates or bowls balanced on boiling pots, etc.

Above all, she will have to acquire the gentle art of knowing when to step in and advise and when to let the girls have the valuable lesson of learning from their mistakes. What does she do, for example, when she sees that a Patrol has no kindling for the morning?

Serving Meals

Patrols sometimes need a little help in understanding that meals should be properly served, with the table set, grace said or sung, food nicely served and eaten in a civilised way, and not a free for all round the fire with fork in hand. For some girls this can be a vital bit of social training. To have a Guider as a guest should help to raise the tone. Wise Guiders encourage their Patrols to acquire plastic tablecloths, which may be the real thing, a yard of plastic from Woolworth's, or mother's ex-kitchen curtains. This ensures that food is neatly and hygienically set out, and discourages the rather tempting abuse of groundsheets.

If Company camping, a Patrol other than cooks is usually delegated to hand round the food, while the cooks serve it up. (The traditional name for this Patrol, borrowed from the army, is Mess Patrol. Guides may wish to stick to this, but others may find it outdated and prefer a name such as waitresses.) If a proper routine is established, serving can be done neatly and quickly. Out-of-doors, food tends to get cold very quickly, so speed, especially if there is a large number to be served, is essential and efficiency should not be hampered by senseless traditions or outdated etiquette.

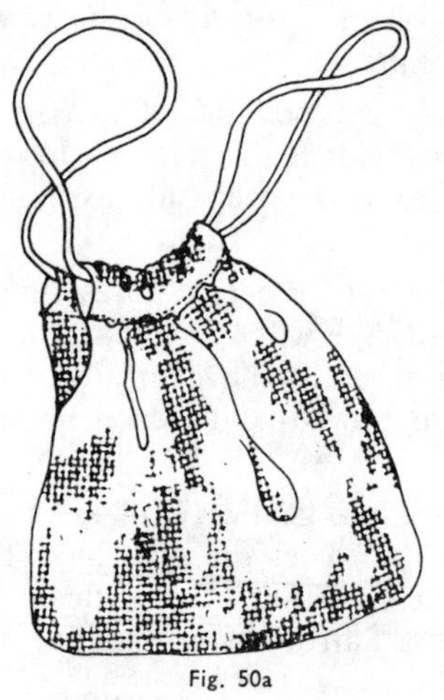

Fig. 50a

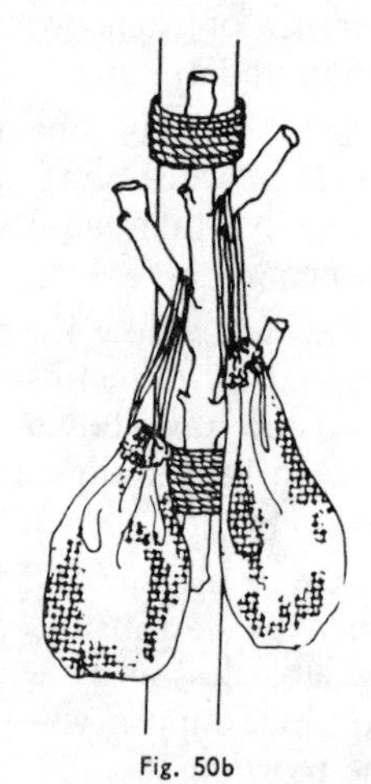

Fig. 50b

It is usually found best if everyone has her dishes and cutlery in a drawstring bag (Fig. 50) with each item named or otherwise identifiable by the owner. (A really effective way of marking dishes is hard to find, though some swear by Trichem paint and others by Fablon-type name-tapes.) After washing up is done, dishes and cutlery are returned to their bags.

NOTE: Hot pans, etc. should never be placed directly on the grass. Two logs or bricks make an adequate pot-rest. Lids should be put upside-down on the grass and replaced immediately if there is any food left in the pan. If empty pans are immediately filled with water, cleaning them later will be much easier.

Washing Up.

Patrols with 4·5 litre-can fires (see p. 58) are at an advantage here as they do not have to make the effort to remember to put on washing-up water. Otherwise, a kettle or water-boiler put on a well-stoked fire when the meal is taken off will usually provide the required hot water at the right time—for all but the very long of tongue!

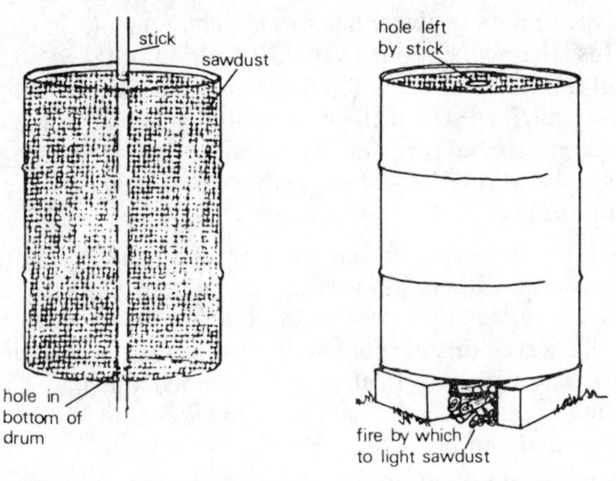

Fig. 51a

Fig. 51b

Even with Company camping washing up is best done in Patrols. For large numbers camping this way the hot water supply is not so simple, as the required amount of water will take longer to heat. If there is no room on the cooking fire a separate fire may be needed for the hot water bin or urn, or a sawdust bin can be used (Fig. 51).

Edible food scraps will be kept for deserving pigs or hens in the locality. Then it is a question of really hot water and detergent. (A note for the inexperienced: liquid detergent bottles empty at an alarming rate in the hands of young Guides, so an allocation of soap powder in a jar or tin may prove more thrifty!) Clean dishmops or cloths and clean tea towels, with efficient scourers for the pots are also needed. (Guides often need reminding that they do not clean camp-fire blackened pots in good polythene wash-up basins.)

As mentioned earlier, wash-up tables make the job much quicker, much easier, and much more hygienic.

Disposal of Waste

Food scraps (if not usable) are put in the pig or hen bucket. Find out and broadcast the fads and fancies of the recipient first. If there is no such home for scraps, they should, if at all possible, be burnt or buried. Unless refuse bins for local collection are available on the site or the site owner has special requirements on the matter, any refuse that will not burn should be buried or taken home. Tins and foil should be burnt out and battered flat, before being put in the refuse pit. The size of the pit required depends on the number of campers. Especial care must be taken with polythene bags. They must not be allowed to blow away. An animal can die as the result of eating one.

Water for disposal, if free from scraps, can be scattered on rough ground. Otherwise it must be poured through a grease trap. A tin with many holes in the bottom (made with hammer and nails) serves this purpose well. It is placed on rough ground and moved every day. It should be cleaned out daily, and this task is made easier if it is lined with bracken, etc., which catches the scraps and can be burnt.

Patrols should be encouraged to devise pre-camp games to help new campers to become familiar with disposal arrangements.

For small touring camps a supply of polythene bags to convey rubbish to the nearest litter bin may prove a better arrangement than trying to bury it with inadequate implements.

Hygiene in the Camp Kitchen

A basin, soap, and towel should be available for cooks to wash their hands—and should be used! Bore a hole through a cake of soap (it must be a fairly hard variety), put a string through, and attach to wash-up table.

There is no need for dirty tea towels or dishcloths in camp! New campers may need some advice on pan-cleaning (see above). Utensils must be thoroughly washed and dried after use. It is handy to have a sheet of foam rubber or polythene on which to lay dishes as they are dried.

Pan lids should be kept on pans as much as possible to protect food from flying ash, and all food should be kept covered. If lids are temporarily removed they should be placed upside down, otherwise they may collect foreign matter on the rims. A wise cook has a plate beside her on which she can lay any implements she is using.

Stores

Ordering Stores

For a standing camp where large numbers are involved it is advisable to visit the shopkeepers in advance. (Guiders who have used the camp-site before, or the local farmer, will be able to supply the names of the shopkeepers, dairy, etc.). Such a visit will establish what the shops can supply (many village stores are surprisingly versatile in their range of goods), if and when deliveries can be made or their van comes round. Often shops that seem hesitant about delivering are quite willing to do so when they hear the numbers involved. When orders are large, it is wise, and courteous, to give the shops good warning of the initial requirements. An advance indication of further requirements during the camp, especially of such things as vegetables, bread, and other perishable foods, is advisable, for your sake as well as the shopkeeper's.

Many Guiders find it a good idea to look out for bargain offers of non-perishable goods and lay in a stock before going to camp.

The secret of efficient ordering is to be continually two jumps ahead, for the first half of the camp to see you have enough, for the second half to see you are not going to be left with a large quantity of surplus stores.

Points for the inexperienced:

Some shops will take back certain untouched goods; it is worth asking.

When Patrol camping take stock of Patrol basic stores before putting in your last grocery order.

Have a few empty containers to collect surplus tea, sugar, and other dry goods which will keep, that Patrols may have left over. A good home for other scraps (butter, margarine, lard, etc.) can usually be found either locally or among the Guides. ('Can you use these up when baking, it's a pity to waste them' may be the tactful line.)

For mobile camps stores will, of course, be bought as required, and according to method of transport. It is wise to find out in advance about early closing day, and in Scotland about local holidays. Many public camp sites, if these are being used, have shops for the convenience of campers.

Quantities. An otherwise wonderful camp can be completely spoiled for many Guides if the food is poor or inadequate. Most teenagers have hearty appetites which camp life does nothing to diminish.

Inadequate food leads to Guides eating more sweets, and it is cheaper in the long run, quite apart from the obvious health element, to charge a little more for camp and provide good food. The cost of sweets to fill the gaps is more than that of increased rations of protein all round. Full consultation with the girls on all food matters usually enables them to appreciate this. Discussions can also be held with parents if they feel that the camp is costing too much.

Large bread consumption is also (though not always) suspect, the indication being that the girls have empty corners to fill up. (Occasionally you get a 'bread-eater' in camp who infects the others and knocks out calculations.) The weather, too, can affect bread-eating. As a result, it is sometimes difficult to calculate the amount of bread required, as it can vary considerably from camp to camp even with the same girls. So it is wise, after the initial order, to indicate probable rather than actual needs, remembering too, of course, that consumption does tend to rise by about the end of the second day.

Knowing how much to order can worry an inexperienced Q.M. The first camp is, of course, the trickiest, so help is given below. If, however, you keep a note of your orders from camp to camp, year to year, you will have a basis to work on.

'I suppose I did order twelve packets of matches'

Catering for Patrol camping is easier as you can think in terms of one Patrol of five or six and then multiply by the number of Patrols concerned.

The following list may help new campers until they establish their own camp-stores-ready-reckoner.

Milk: 450 ml. per head per day—more if milk pudding is on the menu.
Tea: 225 g. per Patrol per week—less if coffee is used also.
Coffee: Amount will depend on how often it is made. It is best to buy a large tin and divide out in small quantities.
Sugar: 340 g. to 450 g. per head per week.
Jam: Amount will depend on nature of meals.
Butter/Margerine: 1–1·25 kg. per Patrol per week (depending on bread consumption).
Bread: Not more than 1 large, sliced loaf per Patrol per day (see note above).
Bacon: 225–340 g. per Patrol per meal.
Sausages: 450 g. per Patrol per meal (sausage meat usually goes further).
Meat: Mince 450–550 g. per Patrol, other meats rather more.
Cold Meat: 340–450 g. approx. per Patrol per meal.
Potatoes: 1–1·25 kg. per Patrol per meal.

Other items will depend on menu.

Basic foods which should be included in initial order:

Salt, pepper, gravy browning, cooking fat, biscuits, cereal, cocoa or chocolate, squash or lemonade crystals, flour, detergent (powder is thriftier than liquid with Guides), Brillo soap pads, scouring powder, matches (2 boxes per Patrol) (Patrol camping is hard on this), toilet rolls.

It is always wise to go through the menu in detail and check with the order, otherwise things like salad cream may be forgotten.

Notes on Buying Stores

Bread: Wrapped, sliced bread is a little more expensive but may prove thriftier in the long run. Guides should be encouraged to eat a proportion of brown bread, as it is more wholesome. (This can be linked up with health.)

Margarine and Butter: For the most part Guides are just as happy eating margarine as butter and it is cheaper. Guiders, however, may well prefer to pay a little more for the privilege of eating butter. (Many *can* tell the difference!).

Buying in bulk. It is thriftier, when dealing with numbers, to take advantage of bulk buying. Shops which supply hotels, etc., often have a range of catering sizes, e.g. jam in 3 kg. tins, which will prove thriftier, provided, of course, that such a quantity is required.

Sizes. When ordering tins, jars, packets, etc. it is wiser to give the weight rather than just to say 'large'. They may have a 'large' size five times as big as you mean. This could prove awkward. A walk round your local store, or consultation with the grocer, will provide you with the weight information you require.

Notes on Storing Certain Foods

Dry foods should be kept in tins (e.g., 3 kg. jam tins with lids) or polythene containers. Meat, sausages, fresh fish, etc. should be cooked the day they are bought. Perishable food should be kept in a larder hung in the shade of a tree. If there is no such shade a buried biscuit tin or dixie makes a good larder for meat and other perishable goods. Mobile camps require careful shopping/menu plans.

Soap powders, etc. should be stored well away from food, and strong smelling items such as onions and smoked fish well segregated. Butter, milk and tea particularly pick up a neighbouring smell very readily.

Milk can be kept (well anchored) in a stream or in a bucket of water in the shade. Any receptacle to be used for milk should be scalded with boiling water, otherwise before long the milk will turn sour.

Green vegetables can be kept in the shade in the grass, if unlikely to tempt the wild life of the neighbourhood. Lettuce keeps fresh longer in a pan with a lid on. Other vegetables can be hung in string bags in a cool place.

All food must be covered. A stock of butter muslin is handy for this can be boiled for re-use. It is important to see that food is inaccessible to whatever livestock the district is liable to produce, from flies to curious cows. A drinking water supply should be kept separate from water for general use. (Patrols camping as such, will generally keep their own.) A water carrier with a stopper is good for this, but if a bucket has to be used it must, of course, be covered, and a hygienically-placed dipper provided (Fig. 52).

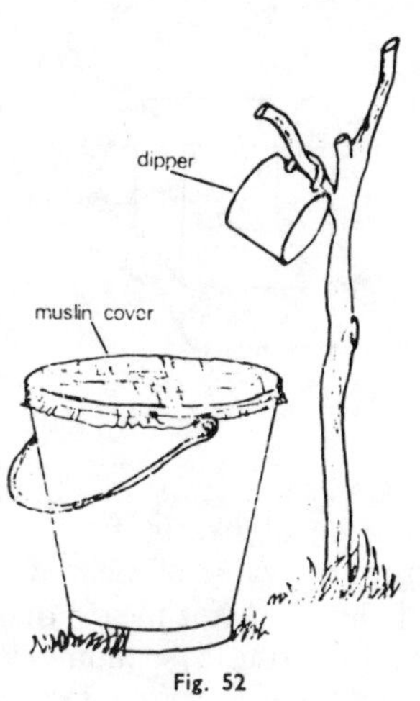

Fig. 52

Miscellaneous Extras

Haybox or Hole. This is a handy device for keeping things hot or for continuing to cook them slowly. It may be useful for Sunday lunch, or supper after a day out. If using a box, line it with paper first, then fill with hay. A hole is simply filled with hay. The pot (which should, of course, have a tight-fitting lid) is then transferred to it at boiling point, covered with a cushion of hay, and a lid. When using it for cooking, cook meat for at least ½ hr., pudding, etc., 15 minutes first and allow at least three times as long as for normal cooking.

Ovens. Some Guides (or Guiders) may like to experiment with camp ovens, cooking in holes, etc., and camp gives a marvellous opportunity for trying these out. The oven illustrated is fun to try or one you have read about elsewhere, or better still one of your own invention (Fig. 53).

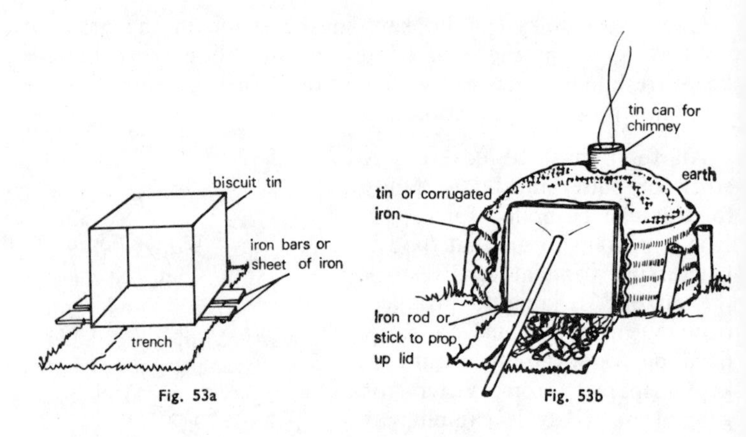

Fig. 53a

Fig. 53b

Canteen. In standing camps it is often a good idea to run a canteen of sweets, fruit, crisps, lemonade, and postcards. Apart from the value of a camp where Guides learn to live independent of shops, etc., it means that sweet consumption can be controlled by imposing a spending limit. Goods can usually be obtained from the grocer on a sale or return basis. If debts are recorded in a book each day, and the total paid either by means of a deposit at the beginning with change given out at the end, or by settling debts at the end of camp, it will cut down the administration and lost coins considerably. Those new to the job are warned that it is wise to charge for lemonade bottles until returned.

Storing Kitchen Equipment

All utensils should be thoroughly dried off (it is sometimes difficult to do this in a wet strike) and stored in a dry place.

Postscript 1: Overheard. 'This Q.M's super. She tells us what to do and then leaves us to get on with it.'

Postscript 2: The most valuable piece of equipment for camp cooking is a sense of humour—whatever happens!

Chapter 6.

TOWARDS HEALTHY CAMPS

Happiness and health! Happy camps are undoubtedly the healthiest. When Guides are busy, and enthusiastic about the ploys in hand, when adventures and exciting activities abound, there is a general feeling of well-being. So the first essential of a healthy camp is a satisfying programme. Where the Patrol system is really working, as in Patrol camping, every Guide has a chance to matter, to feel she is important in some way. This feeling of being 'somebody' in the eyes of others does much to prevent homesickness and other signs of a need for attention. One new Commissioner at her first camp was amazed at the way the older girls looked after the younger ones. 'That's what the Patrol system is all about', she was told.

Common sense psychology plays a large part in keeping a camp healthy. One Guider, having camped, for reasons of economy, some years without a first aid tent (knowing she could 'double up' staff in an emergency) proudly acquired one. She had five clients for it in a week's camp. Next year it was called the 'spare' tent and remained unoccupied! This does not mean that arrangements for dealing with sickness should not be made. On the contrary, the Guider is responsible for other people's children, so she must know what to do and have the wherewithal to do it. But the more the arrangements are advertised, as in all advertising, the more clients she is likely to have.

For every camp there should be one member of staff responsible for health matters, in a large camp preferably not the Guider in charge. The girls should know that she is the one to whom all accidents and sickness are reported. To give her the formal title of Camp Nurse or Camp First Aider, however, is probably a mistake, as it implies that sickness and accidents are expected. Her role should be, as far as possible, to promote health in a positive way, although she must, of course, be qualified to deal with any accident or sickness that may occur. Her job includes keeping an eye on the hygiene in the camp, checking toilet and washing facilities and refuse disposal, and keeping a watchful eye in wet weather. She is a vital member of the camp team, as health is not a separate thing but an integral part of all aspects of camp life.

Food and Health

In the previous chapter the need for a balanced diet has been discussed. For many it may be an introduction to the effects of food on health, and can be a valuable lesson which will be learned by practice rather than by precept. With regard to food fads, girls should know before camp that these cannot be catered for. A rule that works very well is that everyone must eat at least a spoonful of everything unless it is something to which she is genuinely allergic in some way. Many a girl has overcome a food fad in this way, and has learned how much easier life is if one can eat anything. A girl who persistently refuses to eat protein or vegetables or some other item necessary for a balanced diet can often be miraculously cured by saying 'No sweets' or 'You can't buy anything from the canteen until you have eaten a reasonable portion'. Girls usually co-operate well if they have had a say in planning the menu, and especially if they have cooked the food themselves.

It is natural for sweet consumption to be rather above normal in camp, as much more energy is used up and has to be replaced by energy-giving foods. A wise Guider, however, tries to put some sort of control on sweet eating by limiting the amount of pocket money, running a camp canteen with certain restrictions, etc. Parcels from well-meaning parents and friends may create problems, and it is wise to talk this over in advance with parents. While it is nice for all the girls to have a few extras, these should be a supplement to existing meals and not for guzzling at all times of the day and night, so individual parcels should be discouraged, and parents asked to co-operate in the interests of their daughter's health.

The Q.M. and person in charge of health will work together over such matters as drinking water supply, hygienic food handling, and disposal of kitchen waste.

Sanitation

Chemical Toilets

For standing camps many Companies have chemical toilets, which are more hygienic and pleasant to use, and much less likely to cause constipation than trench latrines. Various kinds are available on the market and there is a choice of chemical fluids that have to be used with this type of sanitation. These are available in gallon size containers and should be used according to directions.

If funds will not rise to proper toilets, oil drums with seats (old ones can often be acquired for nothing) will serve the purpose. These drums should be fitted with handles for carrying and when in use should, if large, not be allowed to become more than half full, otherwise there will be difficulty in emptying them. All chemical toilets should be emptied before they become too full, and the seats wiped daily with disinfectant. Soft, soluble toilet paper must be used.

A pit is required, reasonably near the toilets to empty them into, the size depending on the length of the camp, numbers of campers, and drainage. If the latter is good, a pit approximately 1 m. square and $\frac{1}{2}$–1 m. deep will last for a week's camp for 30. After emptying, allow some time for drainage, then sprinkle a very little earth in. The pit should be covered—a piece of corrugated iron makes a good cover but one can be improvised with branches. A warning of its presence may be advisable for the unwary. The pit is filled in at the end of the camp and the sods, which should have been carefully kept and watered daily, replaced.

Trench Latrines

If a trench latrine has to be used, it will probably be necessary to obtain someone locally to dig the trench. For anyone new to this job careful instructions on the width of the trench will be necessary. It should not be more than 30 cm. wide, with the earth thrown clear to one side to allow space for feet on either side of the trench. The length of trench will depend on the size and number of cubicles, allowing 1·25 m. per cubicle, and if about 1 m. deep should last a week. To keep trench latrines sweet, excreta should be covered with soil. A trowel or shovel must be provided for this purpose in each cubicle. Disinfectant is not necessary, but wood ash is good. At the end of the camp the trench must be filled in and the sods replaced. (Fig. 54).

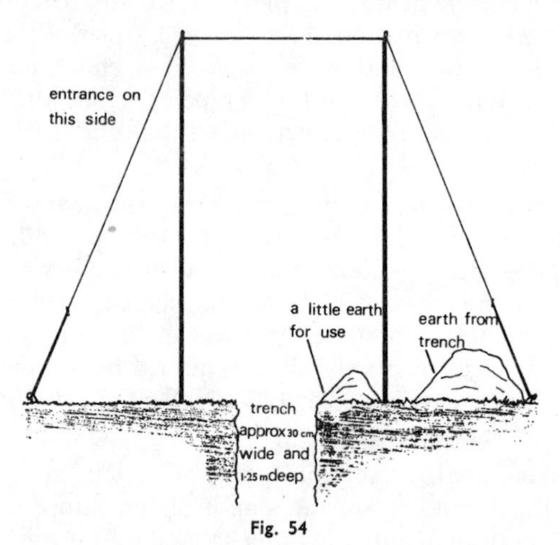

Fig. 54

Position. All toilets should be placed as discreetly as possible. With chemical toilets tree cover can be used, but this is not always possible with trenches because of roots. Ideally they should be to 'leeward' of the tents, near enough to be reasonably accessible, but not so near as to make their presence known. (Trench lats should be at least 50 m. away.)

Trench lats and disposal pits should not be dug where they are likely to foul a water supply or stream.

Cubicles

The type of screening or cubicles chosen will depend on circumstances or finances, but there should be at least one cubicle for every eight people in camp, ideally one per Patrol.

The essential feature of any arrangement is privacy, otherwise the health of sensitive girls may suffer. Individual cubicles, for this reason, are most popular. Single and double cubicles can be bought ready to erect. To do this is simply a matter of putting in poles, putting guylines on poles, and pegging them out.

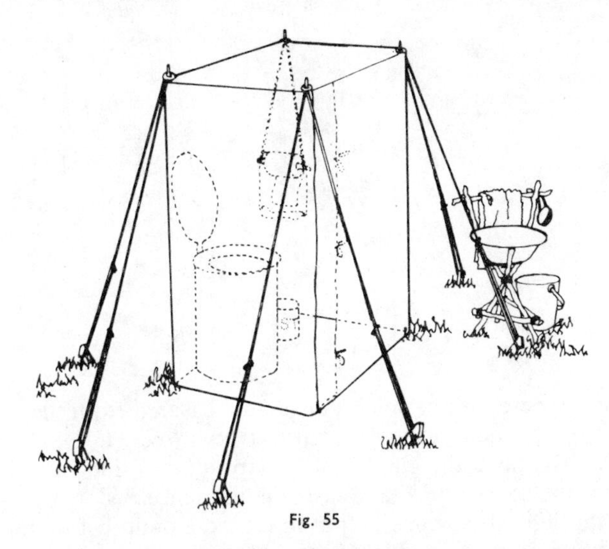

Fig. 55

Screening cubicles can be made with hessian, poles, ropes, and pegs. For a **single cubicle** you require a minimum of 4·5 m. of 2 m. wide hessian, 4 spiked 2 m. poles, a double guyline for each corner and 8 pegs. Poles are placed in a square about 1 m. apart (depending on length of hessian). There should be loops at the top of the hessian where the four corners are to be (Fig. 56). Slip these loops over the spikes of the poles, put on the guylines and peg out, each pair at right angles. Two toggles and loops at the doorway will make a good fastening (Fig. 57). A roof of strong waterproof material made to fit may be added.

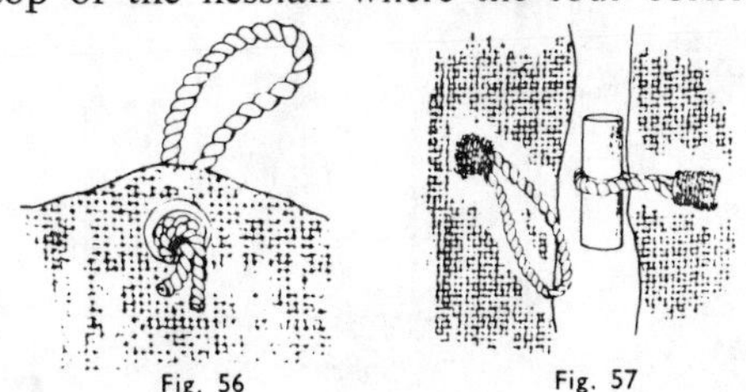

Fig. 56 Fig. 57

A **double cubicle** requires 7·5–9 m. of 2 m. wide hessian (or more—see below), 6 spiked 2 m. poles, 2 ropes approximately 8 m. long, and 3 ropes 6–7·5 m. long. It takes a minimum of four people to erect these. One effective way of doing this is to mark the

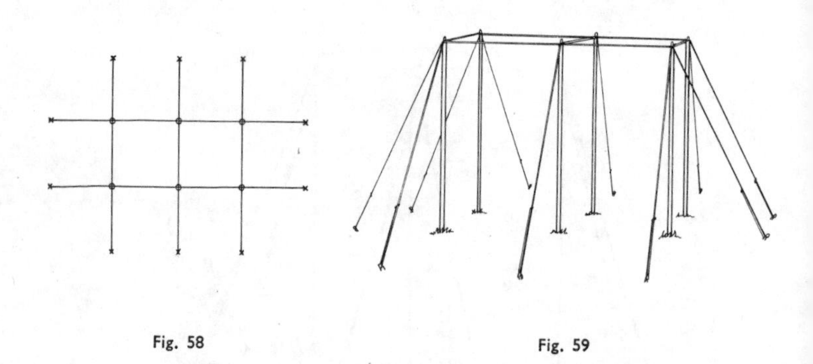

Fig. 58

Fig. 59

positions where the six poles will stand measured from the width of the hessian cubicle, and put in six pegs (see Fig. 58). Three people then hold the three poles in position while the fourth attaches the ropes (see Fig. 59). If the hessian has slots for poles to go through, these must be put in on the ground before raising (see Figs. 60a and 60b). If this is not the case the poles and ropes can probably be put up first and hessian attached afterwards.

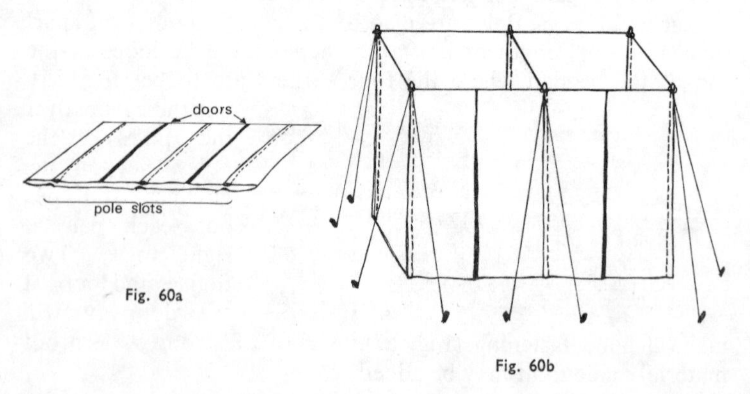

Fig. 60a

Fig. 60b

Care of cubicles. If cubicles have roofs these should be taken off in fine weather, or if they are not removable, the door should be kept looped back. If flies are troublesome, a fly spray should be used.

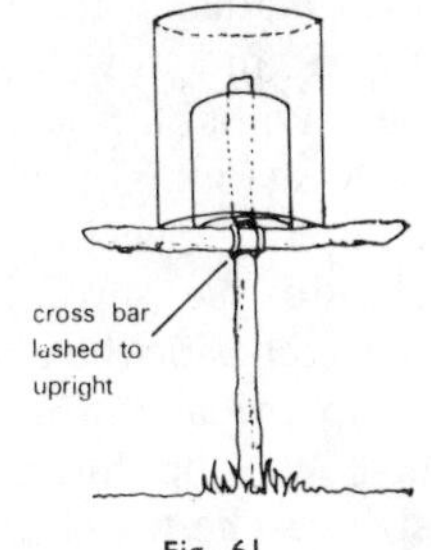

Fig. 61

Equipment for a toilet cubicle consists of toilet paper, some means of holding it (a tin is best if the cubicles are unroofed), an 'engaged' sign, a receptacle for sanitary towels and bags to wrap them in. If Patrol camping, Patrols often dispose of their own in their own fires and prefer it this way. Guides should know, before camp, what the arrangements are. If wood fires are not used, some type of incinerator will be required, as even 'soluble' ones should not be put in chemical toilets.

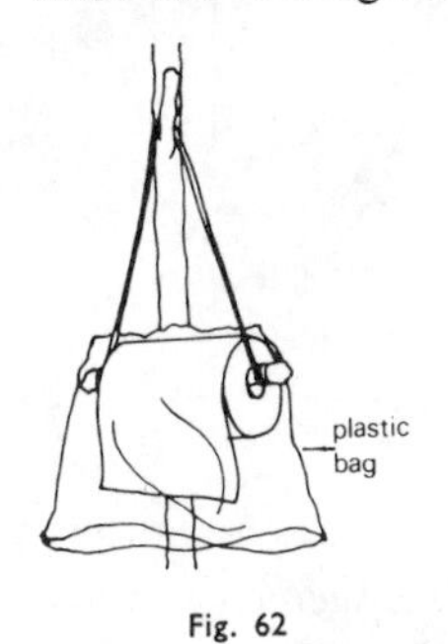

Fig. 62

Generally one Patrol is responsible each day for maintaining toilets or latrines in a hygienic condition, unless each Patrol has its own. In Guiders' camps it is probably not necessary to make this a formal duty. With Ranger camps the need will depend on the age and experience of the Rangers and the type of camp.

Sanitation in Lightweight Camps

For overnight, or lightweight mobile camps, where public camp-sites with 'facilities' are not being used, it is advisable to dig a small latrine trench. If weight is not a problem Rangers may want to take some sort of portable screen. If not they will have to make use of any available cover. In this case a sharp trowel should be sufficient for the necessary digging. Care should be taken to avoid possible pollution of streams. Where transport is available, collapsible chemical toilets and lightweight toilet tents could be used—finances, of course, permitting! Packs of toilet paper or tissue will be found easier than rolls to carry. Arrangements for disposal of sanitary towels will have to be worked out and made known, to avoid embarrassment.

Toilet Hygiene

Whatever arrangements are made, water, soap, basin and towel should be available near the toilets (Fig. 63). In Guide camps especially these should be prominently placed beside the cubicles. Soap (of a hardish variety) can be hung on a string. The towel, if hung on a rail, can be covered with a large polythene bag if it is raining. It should be changed frequently. If disposal is no problem, paper towels in a tin may be found more practical, with a wind proof receptacle for used ones.

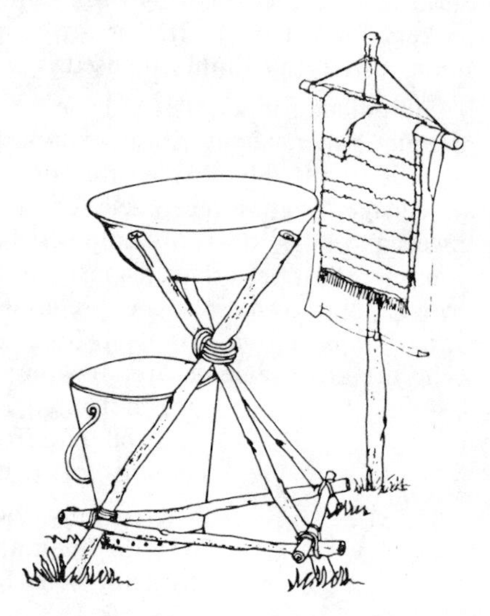

Fig. 63

Washing Facilities

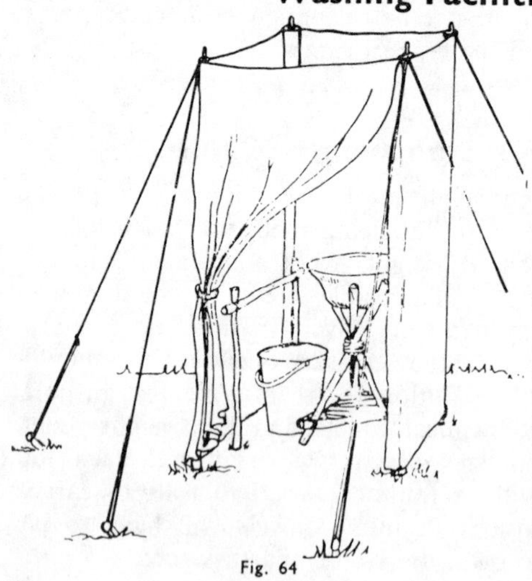

Fig. 64

Arrangements must be made so that girls can wash in privacy. In a standing camp, cubicles such as those described above are generally found best, about one for every 6-8 girls, ideally one per Patrol. If Guides are encouraged to fit out their cubicles with a stand for the basin, towel rail, etc., they will find washing easier and more comfortable (Fig. 64).

Most Companies find the best arrangement is to have a large bin or urn of hot water in the evening. (A dustbin full of water heats up remarkably quickly and provides plenty of water.) Girls can then have a hot wash before going to bed. Guides should know, of course, that they are expected to have an all-over wash every day, and this may be the opportunity to start the habit. Many will value the hint that to wash their feet, even in cold water, before going to bed, as well as being hygienic will ensure that they are warm in bed.

Basins should be kept for use in wash cubicles only, and not mixed with those used for food. Water can be scattered in rough ground after use. Guides should be told to bring tooth mugs to camp. Apart from pointing to the necessity for teeth-cleaning, it may save many cups of toothpaste-tasting tea. Towel rails should be improvised, so that damp towels are not stuffed in kit or mixed up with bedding.

Usually, unless each Patrol has its own cubicle, the Health Patrol attends to keeping basins and cubicles tidy—though this should not be necessary.

Arrangements for Dealing with Sickness

Before Camp

It is advisable for the Guider to meet the girls' parents before camp, partly to reassure them that the girls will be well cared for, and partly to find out if any special precautions have to be taken with regard to their daughter's health. She needs answers to such questions as: May she bathe? Has she started her monthly periods, and if not does she know about them? (Quite often girls start these in camp.) Does she need extra rest at this time? Has she any special weakness, and are there any drugs or foods to which she is allergic? Has she had an anti-tetanus injection recently? These are best brought quietly into conversation; a formal questionnaire might frighten parents off camp for ever!

It is well for the Guider to assure herself that none of the girls has recently been in contact with an infectious disease.

Other information required: Parents' address and phone number for the times of the camp and the girl's National Health number. It can also be very helpful to have the name and address of each camper's home doctor. A health form is obtainable from Guide shops on which this information may be entered.

If girls are to be participating in very strenuous activities, e.g. climbing, as an integral part of the programme, it is advisable, if the girls are not well known to you, to obtain a medical certificate of fitness for such activities.

Before going to camp a doctor in the area should be asked if he is willing to attend the camp if necessary. His address, phone number, and the location of the telephone nearest to the camp should be known to all the camp staff, also the times and place of his surgery.

Equipment

Apart from a spare tent or some other accommodation, it is advisable, in a standing camp, to have available a camp bed, with groundsheet, spare blankets (aired daily), and a hot water bottle. A basin, soap, and towel should be readily available, and is is advisable to have in camp a small stove and kettle or pan for first aid use. Particulars of how to contact the doctor should be prominently displayed. A medicine/first aid box will be required, the contents varying according to individual preferences. The following list may suggest how possible ailments and accidents are to be prepared for.

Equipment	**Possible Uses**
Disprin or similar	Headaches, etc.
Vick, gargle (salt or sod. bic. and water), cough sweets	Sore throat, cold
Andrews Liver Salts	Constipation
Milk of Magnesia, liquid or tablets, or Rennies	Tummy disorder or indigestion
Oil of cloves	Toothache
Optrex or other eye lotion	Spark in eye, sore eye
Calamine lotion or cream	Sunburn
'Sting relief' or anti-histamine cream	Stings—bee, wasp
Dettol, Savlon or T.C.P.	Cuts, grazes, etc.

Cotton wool
Gauze and tubular bandage
Elastoplast
Roll of 1 in. sticking plaster
Crepe bandages
Triangular bandages

General Requirements

- Matches
- Scissors
- Torch
- Safety pins
- Needles (ready sterilised)
- Tweezers
- Small bowl
- Container of fresh drinking water
- Small towels
- Box of tissues
- Medicine glass
- Teaspoon
- Mug
- Clinical thermometer
- Thermos
- Sanitary towels and belt or tape
- Change for phone
- Notebook and pencil
- Up-to-date text-books

Apart from antiseptic lotion and adhesive dressings, small quantities should be bought. Items should be clearly labelled and a list of contents included. Items to be taken internally should be kept separate from those applied externally.

Treating Accident or Sickness

Common sense is the main ingredient of treatment, and a clinical thermometer can often help to distinguish between real illness and desire for attention. Too much sympathy should be avoided until real illness is established. Flapping and fussing are not part of the health expert's stock-in-trade. While one does not wish to burden doctors unnecessarily, it has to be remembered that other people's children are a big responsibility. In cases of severe symptoms combined with raised temperature, a doctor's opinion should be sought. The same applies to suspected fracture or concussion, deep cuts (which may need stitching), or dirty ones (which may require an anti-tetanus injection). If the local hospital has a casualty department, cuts, etc. may be dealt with there, but make sure first, as many of the smaller hospitals have no provision for this. In case of a severe accident it is usually best to summon an ambulance.

No girl should take medicines of any kind without a Guider's permission, and a Guider should not be over-ready to give out aspirins without closely investigating the necd.

Homesickness is sometimes difficult to combat once it has set in. Prevention by means of a full programme, real use of the Patrol system, and, of course, no mention of the possibility of such a thing, is better than a cure. The rest of the Patrol or group can play a large part in helping a homesick girl by keeping her busy and letting her feel needed. Sympathy makes matters worse; often a few sharp words are more effective. However, if a girl, despite all efforts, persists in being miserable, and is spoiling the camp for the others, it may be best to send her home.

Keeping Up to Date. The Guider in charge of health must keep her knowledge of first aid, etc., up to date. The latest manuals of the Voluntary Aid Societies are a very reliable source of information.

General Supervision of Health

It is important to see that the general rules for health are kept in camp. It is a most valuable opportunity to put health training into practice.

Food and hygiene have been dealt with already.

Fresh air and exercise are already 'built-in' and are among the main features of camp life. On the question of fresh air, however, some persuasion may be required to get Guides to leave tent doors open a little during the night to counteract the 'fug' that would otherwise result.

Rest is essential because of the large part that exercise plays in camp life. A period of rest during the day, after lunch often being found to be the best time, can help to counteract overtiredness. Adequate sleep is also essential, and this is sometimes more difficult to achieve. To send the girls to bed too early often has the opposite effect. They will settle down more quickly if really tired and ready for bed. One has to be realistic and take into consideration the time the girls go to bed at home. Guides are, of course, much fonder of their beds in the morning (apart from the first one!). With Patrol camping, when breakfast can be prepared and eaten so quickly, there is really no need to be up much before eight. By consulting the girls about bedtime and rising time, discussing it fully, and letting them feel that their suggestions have influenced the decision, you will find far greater co-operation than by imposing a rule supplied entirely by 'authority'. Persistent nocturnal disturbers of the peace can usually be cured by withholding some privilege (no sweets to be bought in canteen, etc.). Older girls are usually quite sensible about getting the sleep they require and in the main respond to being treated as adults in this way. To impose any curfew on Guiders is, of course, out of the question.

Individual Guides may have to be watched for overtiredness. Such attention should be by means of the watchful eye; fussing and questioning are psychologically bad.

The camp staff, too, should have adequate rest, or frayed edges will appear on tempers. The Guider in charge should keep an eye on her assistants for signs of overwork (and vice versa).

Clothing. Young Guides may not be very sensible about clothing, and may need to be reminded to put on jerseys or jeans if it is chilly, or raincoats if wet. Anoraks are excellent for camp wear, but Guides usually have to be told that they will not generally withstand persistent rain, and that in camp there is no kitchen pulley on which to dry them. In persistent wet weather drying lines may have to be rigged up in the marquee or barn, or a friendly house with a spare pulley found. It is a good idea to get Guides to collect old discarded plastic macs throughout the year, to wear over their anoraks in camp, thus saving their good coats. Gabardines or similar raincoats are not suitable for camp wear, because of the difficulty in drying them and keeping them clean. Rainwear of oilskin, nylon, or plastic is the most suitable.

Gumboots are excellent for rain in camp, but Guides should be discouraged from wearing them when the weather is fine. Plimsolls worn *without* socks are also good in the rain or in wet grass as long as the girls are active. Clogs worn with thick socks, as worn by Dutch Guides, are perhaps the best camp footwear of all, as they give protection and are good for the feet. Wooden-soled exercise sandals are excellent too, worn without socks when the grass is wet. Leather shoes are not practical on the camp-site. For hiking, however, girls must have strong walking shoes or boots, worn with socks, of preferably a wool and cotton mixture. To dry wet shoes or boots try stuffing them with newspaper.

Complete changes of clothing should be brought. No day clothes should be worn at night.

Bedding should be adequate and blankets sewn or folded into a bag. A spare jersey and socks for sleeping in may be brought for cold weather.

Miscellaneous Hazards

Wet weather is the commonest among weather hazards. Apart from aiming to keep the Guides as dry as possible, the secret of combating this hazard is to keep them happily occupied. Their planning for camp should, therefore, include activities for wet days.

Sun in camp is lovely, but too much can be very harmful, so sunbathing must be strictly limited, especially early in the season before the girls are acclimatised. The girls will probably not believe you so some hounding may be necessary. If hiking, cycling, or pony trekking, it may be necessary to alter the schedule and rest in the shade during the hottest hours. High altitudes and places by the sea are the most dangerous spots for sunburn.

Thunder and lightning are generally more frightening than dangerous. Counteract alarm with sing-songs, stories, hilarious fun. Do not shelter under trees, near wire fences, etc., and it is better to sit clear of the tent poles.

Mosquitoes and midges can become a real hazard. Have a plentiful supply of repellent, sprays, etc. Keep as much of the body as possible covered. Be prepared if camping in a notorious area, near woods or water.

Unwelcome visitors (of the two-legged variety!) are scarcely a health problem but may have a real nuisance value. Discuss the problem with the girls and they will usually agree that it is better to ignore the local youths if they seem too interested. Sometimes it works to invite such an audience to come on a conducted tour—ending at the gate! If 'visitors' enter the site and interfere with equipment, the local police should be summoned. Guides should know the boundaries of the camp-site and realise that they just do not go beyond them without permission. If, through a frank discussion, they know why, they will not feel hemmed in or over-subjected to imposed rules and regulations.

Rangers will deal with such problems by means of discussion and will generally decide on a sensible course of action. There may, however, be times when the Guider has to step in rather firmly, if the welfare of the girls in her charge is in jeopardy, or if she feels she would be betraying the trust of their parents by allowing a certain course of action.

Conclusion

The approach to health should be a completely practical, no-nonsense, no-fuss one. Because the welfare of the girls is at stake, certain courses of action must be taken. But, if the girls, through pre-camp discussions, can see the necessity for such actions and impose it on themselves, a valuable training for life will be given, as well as a healthier camp ensured.

The Guider needs great wisdom to bring this about, but a sense of humour helps. It is fun to be healthy too!

Chapter 7.

FURNISHING YOUR CAMP

It is a wonderful challenge to Guides and Rangers to make their camp as comfortable as possible, and they derive tremendous satisfaction from devising and constructing gadgets for this purpose. Mind and hands combine to create something that is actually going to be used, that costs no money, and is made from what can be found around them. For some girls this is their most valuable contribution to camp life, and to have an opportunity and encouragement to make it is satisfying a real need. A sense of proportion, however, is essential to ensure that gadget-making does not become an end in itself to the detriment of other activities.

If the skills required in making gadets are learned and practised by the girls in advance it will help them to construct what they need quickly, as well as provide the incentive to do so.

Choosing the Materials

Natural wood is the obvious choice for camp gadgets. As dead wood is too brittle to be of use, permission will have to be sought to cut green wood. If none is available near the site and transport problems do not exist, Guides may bring trimmed bundles of suitable wood (the result of pre-camp Patrol expeditions). Most sought after is the *forked stick*—the subsequent illustrations of gadgets will show its use. One side of the fork should be a continuation of the branch (Fig. 65a), otherwise it will tend to split when being driven in. Forked ends should be trimmed well down and cut smooth across to avoid damage to the unwary passer-by. Straight sticks trimmed to the required length, and of the thickness suitable for the strain they will have to

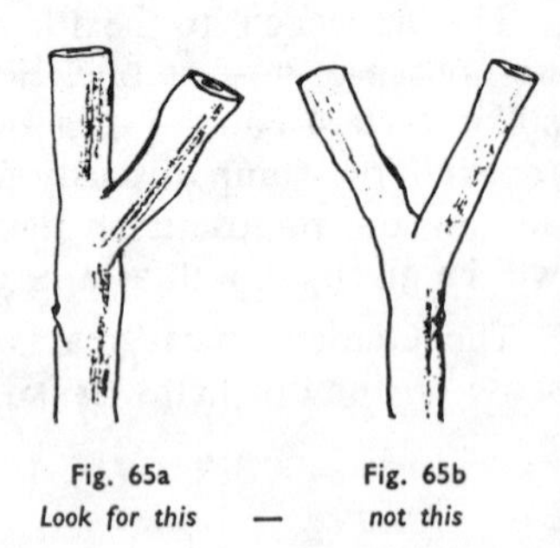

Fig. 65a *Look for this* — Fig. 65b *not this*

take, are the next essential. Bark should be left on for the natural look. Where little or no wood is available, Guides will have to use their ingenuity, and whatever is there. Stones and bricks, if used, should be moved daily, otherwise the grass will be marked. If camping by the shore, there may be driftwood, fish boxes, etc., which will eliminate the necessity for elaborately lashed constructions. Pegs should not normally be used, but broken ones are useful as props. Ingenuity is the keynote of success, and there is no right or wrong way, or material, provided the gadgets are serving the purpose and not likely to do any damage.

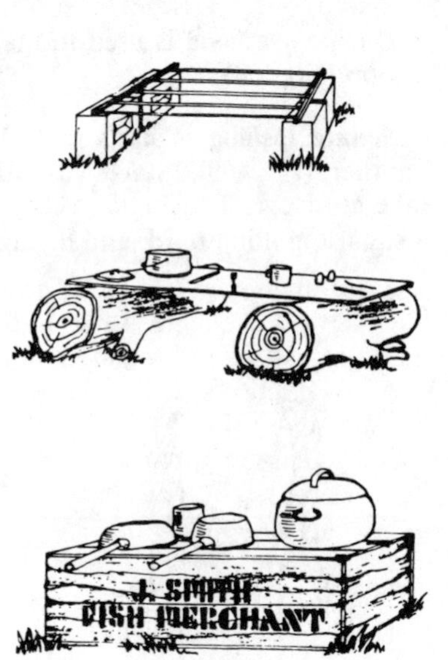

Pot racks devised from materials found on the site

Knots and Lashings which May be Used

Clove hitch is used frequently in camp when tying a rope or cord to a pole or stick when both ends are to be used (Fig. 66).

Round turn and two half hitches is used to tie a rope to a pole when there is strain on one end only (Fig. 67).

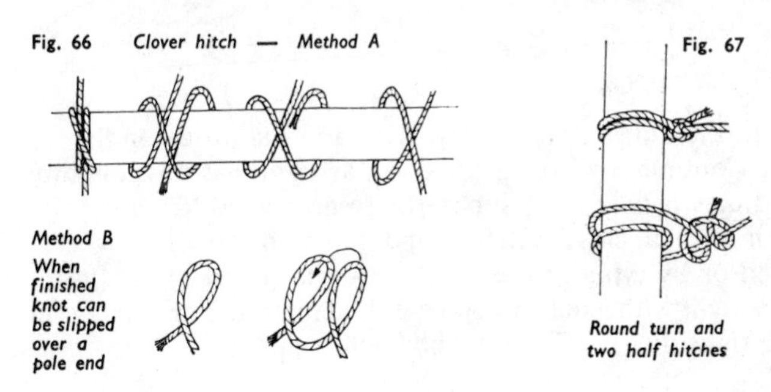

Fig. 66 *Clover hitch — Method A*

Fig. 67 *Round turn and two half hitches*

Double overhand is used to make a loop (Fig. 68).

Fig. 68
Double overhand

Square lashing is used to lash one stick at right angles to another (Fig. 69). Start with the clove hitch round one spar, take cord over first, under second, back over first, continuing in a square, pulling hard, and laying the cord alongside the previous

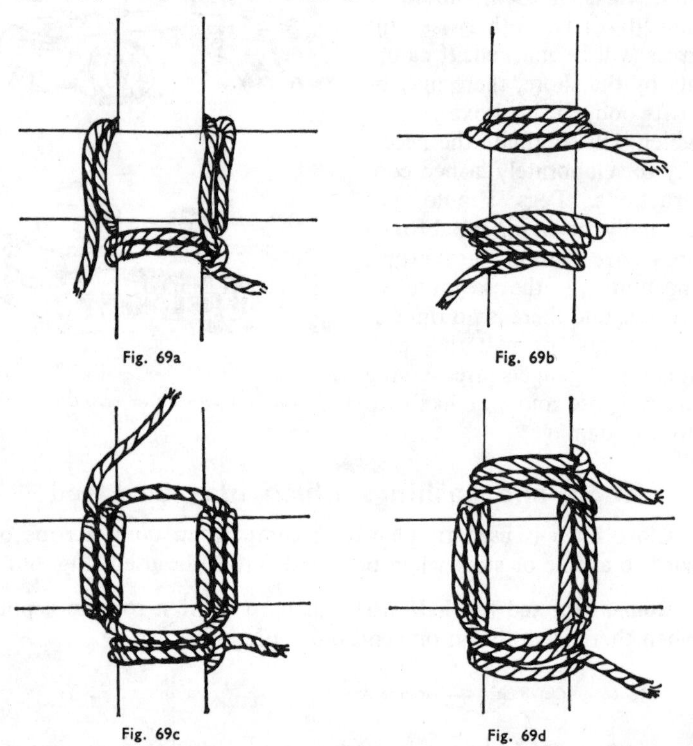
Fig. 69a Fig. 69b
Fig. 69c Fig. 69d

turn to the outside on the first stick and the inside on the second stick. Continue by taking the cord, as tightly as possible three or four times between the sticks (these are called 'frapping turns'). Finish with a clove hitch round the spar opposite where you started or by tying to the other end with a reef knot. Push ends out of sight with a marline spike or knife point. The lashing should be so tight that it will not wobble when pulled.

Tripod lashing is used to make a tripod to support a basin or to replace a forked stick where these àre not available or the ground too rocky to hold them. Lay three sticks of equal length

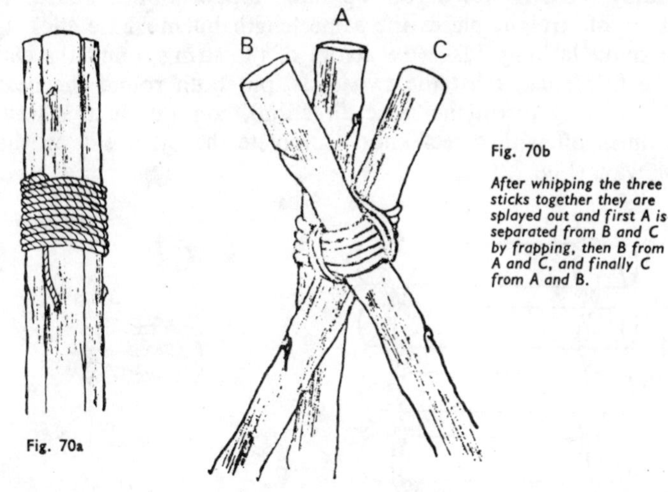

Fig. 70a

Fig. 70b

After whipping the three sticks together they are splayed out and first A is separated from B and C by frapping, then B from A and C, and finally C from A and B.

and thickness side by side. Whip round these sticks, taking in the end of the cord but leaving enough to finish off, for about an inch, not too tightly. Open out the tripod and frap two or three times tightly between each pair in turn. Finish off with a reef knot (Fig. 70).

Snake lashing is a means of making a table top, the top being lashed on to two stout sticks of the required length, and consisting of thinner, straight pieces, all cut the same length. Using the middle of the cord, make a clove hitch round one end of the base stick, having the knot on top. Bring the two ends up and over the first cross piece, down under the 'base' stick, crossing and coming up again. Lay the second cross piece alongside the first and continue lashing each piece on in this way. Lash the crosspieces to the other base

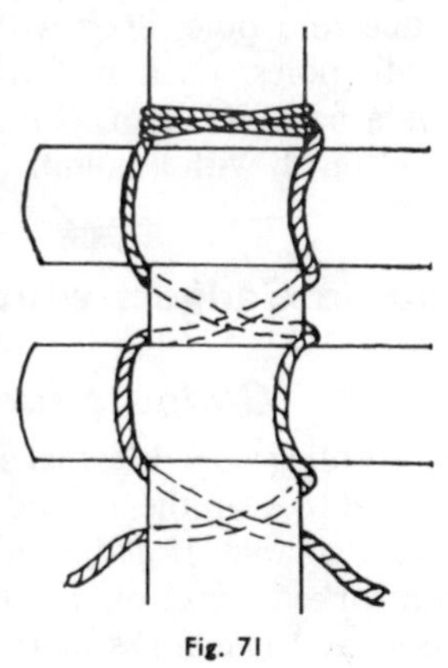

Fig. 71

in the same way. Two people working together can do this very quickly. (Fig. 71).

Malay hitch makes a roll-top table top or notice board. It consists of straight pieces the same length but no base stick as with snake-lashing. Place the centre of the string round the end of the first stick, twist the two ends, put both round the next stick, twist again (in the same direction), continue in this way, and finish off with a reef knot. Complete the other side in the same way. (Fig. 72).

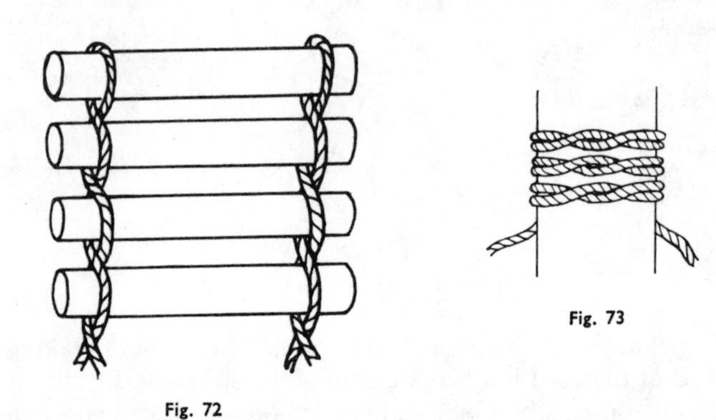

Fig. 72

Fig. 73

West Country whipping is used to join two poles together, e.g. when using two poles to improvise a flagpole, or to lash a stick to a pole. Start with the centre of the cord, bring it round both poles, tie a half reef knot, bring both ends to the back, tie a half reef knot, continue in this way for the required length and finish with a complete reef knot. (Fig. 73).

Some Gadgets which Guides may Wish to Make

Gadgets for the Sleeping Tent

Bedding and kit racks. In a standing camp, kit should be raised to keep the ground in good condition, using what materials are available. If gadget wood is obtainable then a raised platform on forked sticks or tripods is usually most satisfactory. The tent pole and two forks or tripods in V shape also makes a good kit rack. The poles are lashed together on to the tent pole, with the other ends resting on the forks. Where the gadget has to be moved at night, loops can be lashed to the tent pole and the gadget poles inserted through them instead. (Fig. 74).

Framed rucksacks can be placed resting on the two corners of the frame and leaning against a stick driven into the ground.

Individual items can be placed on five improvised pegs of the same height, driven into the ground, one at each corner and one in the middle. Improvised bedding racks might include drift-wood on flat stones, a grid, found nearby, on brick, or an upturned box.

Fig. 74
Rope used double for West Country whipping and loops left hanging at end of whipping to support cross bars

Fig. 75

Towel rail. This is another essential item. Ideally there should be one outside the tent, and one inside (for night and wet weather). One good way of accommodating a number of towels in a hygienic way is illustrated in Fig. 75. A simple rail on two forked sticks is also effective.

Shoe rack is a popular gadget and is very simple to construct (Fig. 76).

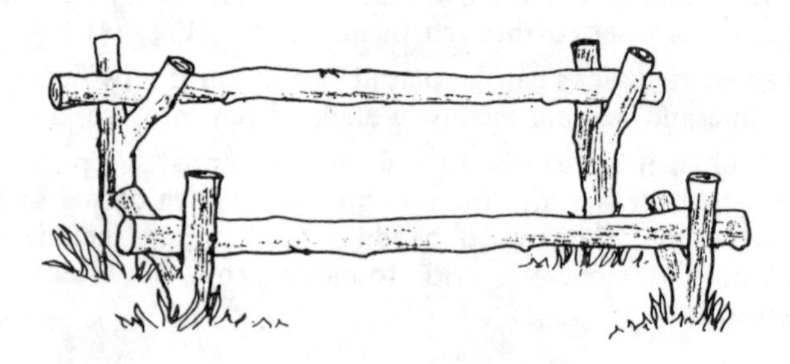

Fig. 76

Gum boots can be placed upside down outside on sticks driven into the ground just high enough to discourage insects from effecting an entry.

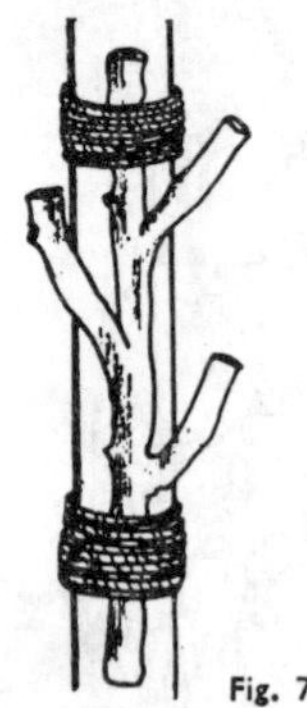

Fig. 77

Clothes hanger. A stick with several forks on it lashed to the pole, top and bottom, with West Country whipping makes a good hanger (Fig. 77). If coat hangers are used (and these should be encouraged to prevent a garment's dry inside coming against a wet outside) a cross piece can be square-lashed to a centre upright, or one where there is a bell-end, above eye level for obvious reasons, but not so high as to rub the canvas. Even the best lashing will protest unless the weight is wisely distributed.

Hold-all. Many Patrols like to have a hold-all, made of material, with pockets for holding things required by all of them: torch, sewing kit, string, etc. This can either be hung from an upright or, with a stick through the top hem, rest on two forked sticks. (Fig. 78).

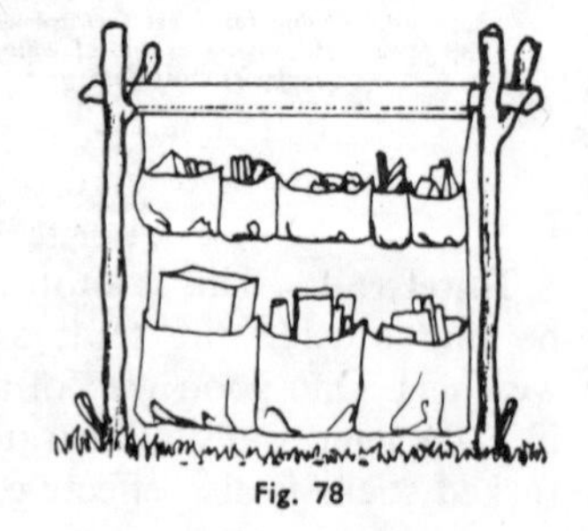

Fig. 78

Kitchen Gadgets

(see Chapter 5).

General Gadgets

Wash tents. A simple washstand, e.g. a tripod, and a towel rail is all that is required.

Flagpole. If improvisation is necessary, join two poles, if one long enough cannot be found, with West Country whipping. Attach to the top a ring, staple, or rope loop through which the halyards can run easily. Make four guylines by using two ropes attached to the pole with clove hitches. Finally, square lash to the pole a stick round which the halyards can be wound. (Fig. 79).

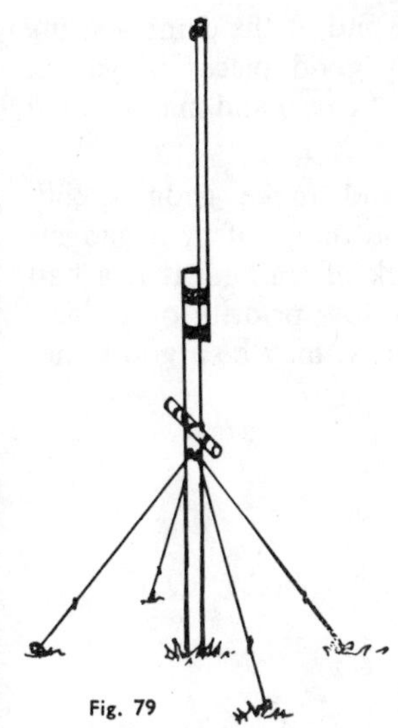

Fig. 79

Lightweight Camps

Rangers, with encouragement, will enjoy improvising 'furnishings', possibly of a totally unorthodox nature, no matter what kind of camp it is. They will quickly develop an eye for things in their surroundings which can be used to make life easier or more comfortable.

Notes on Camp Gadgets

1. Use the best materials available.
2. Point the ends of the forks, etc. with an axe before hitting them in. If you first make a hole with a tent peg, they will go in more easily still.
3. Leave no sharp ends on gadgets where they may do injury to persons or equipment.

4. Make sure your gadget will stand (literally) when subjected to the 'little push' test.
5. Make your gadgets on the first day and enjoy them for the rest of camp.
6. Always dismantle gadgets at the end of the camp—string and all—sad though it is! Any good pieces of gadget wood should be kept at the end of camp and may be used for many more camps.
7. Encourage Guides to devise and make gadgets, but beware of making too much of a 'thing' of it. If gadgetlessness is due to laziness or lack of training it is a bad thing, but if it is because of the low priority of gadget-making in an exciting programme it may be a good one.

Chapter 8.

ORGANISING CAMP LIFE

When numbers of people are involved a certain amount of organisation is necessary. Also, with younger girls especially, they feel more secure and therefore happier if they know just what is expected of them (even if they do not always do it!). No one is happy if just left to muddle through, but, on the other hand, a strict military-like discipline in all matters will lead to conscious or sub-conscious rebellious attitudes, expressed in various ways. Organisation should come as far as possible from within, because the need for it is seen, not as discipline imposed by authority. A system worked out by the Patrol Leaders' Council or Ranger Council is the best way of running a camp.

Another secret of good camp organisation is the delegation of responsibility, having, of course, given the appropriate training for it before camp. It will be apparent from the other chapters of this book that in a Guide camp the role of the Patrol Leader is a vital one, so opportunity must be made before the camp to train each according to her needs, both in the skills involved and in organising and caring for her Patrol. Pre-camp training of Rangers will be geared according to their knowledge and experience and the type of camp they are planning. Local experts in different fields may well help with this training.

The Arrival

A well-planned arrival will give the camp a much happier start. When practical, leave in the morning and arrange for the girls to bring packed food for their first meal. This can be eaten while the Patrols choose their sites and the lay-out is planned.

It is best, practically and psychologically, if the girls first pitch their sleeping tents, put their kit in them, change into camp dress, unless they have travelled in it (which is often more practical than wearing best uniform), then get their own kitchens organised. They are then ready to share, as previously worked out by their P.L.s' or Ranger Council, in general camp pitching. Some sort of time challenge may help to put Guides, especially if they are not your own Company, on their toes, and get the camp off to a flying start.

If it is wet on arrival, kit should be put in shelter, if available, or covered with a few old groundsheets, or put in one tent quickly pitched by the most experienced, suitably clad, until sleeping tents are up.

Other immediate needs are some drinking water (travelling and pitching are thirsty work) and volunteers to pitch one toilet cubicle.

Camp Duties

In Guide camps, as has been mentioned in previous chapters, it is usually found to be most convenient if Patrols take it in turn to perform the general camp chores, while within the Patrol the P.L. works out a similar type of rota.

	Sat	Sun	Mon	Tues	Wed
Cook					
Water					
Wood					
Health					

Fig. 80

A list of duties can be drawn up and divided equally among the Patrols, the division depending on the amount of work involved, e.g. one camp may have a convenient tap, while in

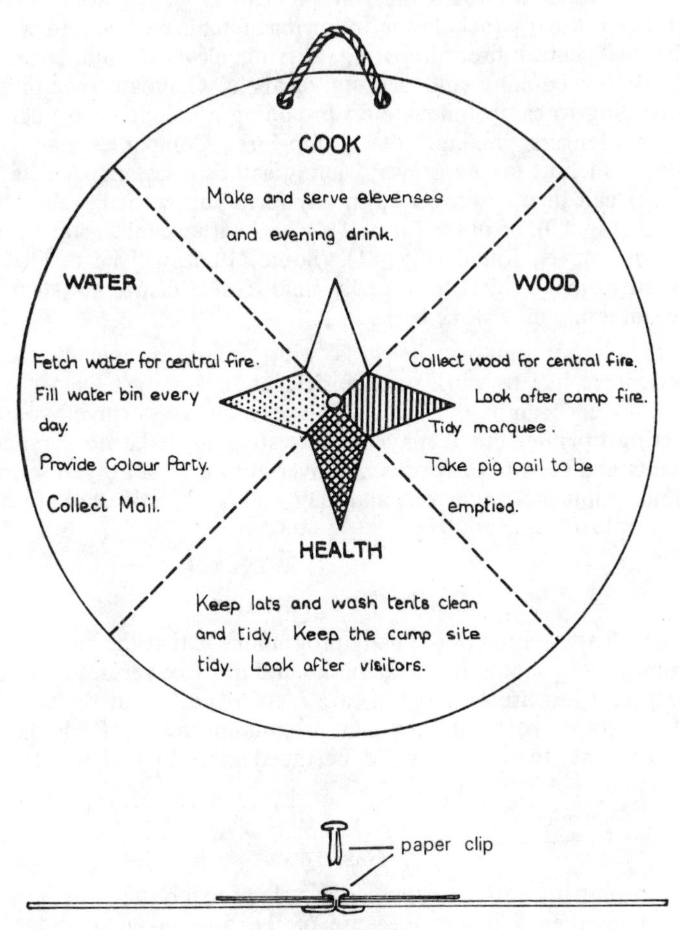

Fig. 81

Star shape is separate and can be changed when the duties change

another water may have to be carried quite a distance, so allocation of other duties to the water Patrol is geared accordingly. Duties normally include the following: fetching wood and water for the central fire; preparing, serving elevenses and evening drink (or cooking and serving meals if Company camping); attending to camp toilets, etc.; providing a colour party; acting as messengers; making the Camp-Fire. Companies may add others such as taking prayers, acting as hostesses, etc. A rota of duties can then be drawn up in any form you wish: in tabulated form (Fig. 80), or in the form of a wheel with a central star which can be moved round (Fig. 81). (Some Guide will be thrilled if asked to make this!) In a really small Guide camp, a system of volunteering may work better.

In Ranger camps, the girls will, unless completely inexperienced, like to work out the delegation amongst themselves. In Guiders' camps the same will apply, or a system of volunteering operate, but it may be interesting to make no arrangements and see what happens. An over-authoritarian organisation is not popular with anyone and may well (and justifiably) appear an insult to some adults.

Daily Programme

The first essential of the daily programme is that the mechanics (timing, etc.) should fit the activities and not vice versa. Sufficient sleep and rest are essential, as are regular meals, but the timing of these can be flexible to suit programme needs. Each day's programme, therefore, should be timed according to the ploys on hand.

Rising

If Company camping the cooks will probably have to be up not later than 7.30 a.m. because of the time taken to prepare breakfast. If Patrol camping, when breakfast can be quickly made for the smaller number, 8.00 a.m. may be early enough. Experienced campers can be even later. 'If you guarantee to have a proper breakfast, beds aired, tents and kitchens tidy, and your camp duties done by 10.30 a.m. you can get up when you like' said one Guider. And they did!

Inspection

10.30 or 11.00 seems a reasonable time to expect Guides to have everything ship-shape, and it is understood, of course, that it remains that way all day. A time-tabled formal inspection should not be necessary and tends to encourage putting on a show for a brief period and not bothering for the rest of the day. A detailed inspection in Guide camps the first day at a pre-arranged time is useful, and thereafter all that is necessary is the knowledge on the part of the Guides that you are expecting them to be tidy and careful, and *are noticing that they are*. With new campers a few spot checks can be made to keep them on their toes, or some form of token given out to them when a high standard is achieved. Encourage the attitude, however, that tidiness is a matter of pride, not something just to please authority. Guiders and Rangers should not be inspected but given any constructive help they require in a manner suited to their age and experience.

Meals

Meals, of course, are frequently highlights in the camp day, as girls are usually especially hungry in camp, and while their timing should be flexible, too long a gap between them may lead to the eating of too many sweets. On an expedition a packed snack can be taken, either a fairly adequate one for lunch, or simply biscuits, chocolate, and fruit for a longish afternoon one. Sometimes tea and a snack, and supper about 7 p.m. will suit the programme best; sometimes it is better to have a high tea about 6 p.m. When Patrol camping, Guiders usually prefer to make their own breakfast, but go as guests to the Patrols, in turn, for one or both main meals.

Colour Ceremonial

In a standing camp it is usual to have a flagpole and hoist Colours every day. (For improvising a flagpole see Chapter 7. Directions for hoisting Colours appear in *The Guide Handbook*.) The symbolism attached to this ceremony has extra meaning and appeal in camp. The flag may be hoisted and/or lowered by a colour party alone, with a whistle blown so that everyone stands at attention while it is broken or lowered. If all the girls are to be present, they can work out themselves beforehand how the ceremony is to be performed. As long as it is carried out with dignity and respect, a simple ceremony, usually with the Company standing in horseshoe formation, is all that is needed. Caps are usually worn for the ceremony, and campers should be tidy.

Either the World Flag or the Union Flag may be flown. If visitors from another country are in camp, either the World Flag or the flag of the visitors' country should be flown alongside the Union Flag (not below it on the same pole).

The flag may be hoisted before breakfast, but if the whole Company is to be present, after breakfast when everyone is free to attend is generally found to be convenient. Standing for a time, breakfastless, is sometimes a strain.

As, by tradition, Colours should not be left unguarded, they should be taken down in the evening and also if the camp is being left unoccupied during the day.

Prayers

(See Chapter 10).

Patrol Leaders' Council

In a Guide camp, this will probably take place every day, to report on how things are going, on any individual needs, and to plan for the next day. It need not be a very formal meeting unless the girls wish it that way.

Ranger Council

At a standing camp, Rangers often meet together informally in Council each day to assess how things are working out and to adjust plans accordingly. They may meet regularly in mobile camps, too, where there is a need for day by day planning. At a Ranger/Scout camp, representative members of each Movement normally meet daily as a Joint Council.

Programme of Activities, Camp-Fire, etc.

(See Chapter 9)

Rest Hour and Free Time

Provision should be made for these each day whenever possible.

Bedtime

There should be a quiet final activity, or quiet ending to Camp-Fire, a hot drink and biscuit, a hot wash, and time to chat before the Lights Out signal is given—at an hour agreed as reasonable by the Patrol Leaders' Council.

Rangers will usually appreciate an appeal to their common sense rather than a curfew. Guiders can please themselves!

While flexibility in the time-table makes for a happy camp, punctuality when times are fixed should be given top priority, out of common courtesy.

Dress

Girls of Guide age tend to act the part of the clothes they are wearing, and really do feel more Guide-like when wearing some form of uniform. As camp uniform is also practical, it is wise to insist on the wearing of it. Navy shorts or jeans and blue shirt are comfortable, and can also be used by girls when not Guiding. For hot days the Guide camp dress is cool and practical. Many Companies keep a stock of these (either bought or made by themselves). If each girl has a camp dress which can be kept reasonably tidy, it may be possible to dispense completely with best uniform in camp, especially at a week-end.

Common-sense must be used when deciding what to wear and when, taking into consideration, after cleanliness and tidiness are ensured, such factors as the weather, the activity, and what might offend an observer. For example, if Guides were being shown round a neighbouring castle, or invited to visit local Guides, it would be rather discourteous to be casually dressed in shorts or jeans, but it is doubtful if the local cows or sheep, a passing motorist, or even the village grocer, would be offended to see girls in jeans. Indeed they would look far more out of place on a country road in full uniform and detergent-white socks!

Hair should be kept as tidy as possible, as weather permits, and if long, should be tied back. Rollers should not be allowed to appear in public. Aprons should be removed for meals. A lot of useful social training can be quietly given in this way.

Rangers will choose the clothes most suitable for the activity on hand, not necessarily uniform. The choice of clothes may well be part of the preparation for camp, or of some session on dress sense. Common-sense, based on weather, programme, and social acceptability, will again be the basis for a any decision.

As a general rule there is little need for Guiders (or Rangers) to take their uniform jackets and skirts to camp. The Guider's short sleeved uniform dress is official wear for all summer occasions. For informal events there is the Guider's camp dress (with or without sleeves) that may also be worn by Rangers, and which is cool and comfortable in hot weather. Shorts and shirts may be worn on the site if preferred by those with suitable figures. Jeans and slacks are sensible camp wear for chilly days and midgy evenings, and equally appropriate for walking or other outdoor activities.

A navy or Guide blue windcheater or anorak is probably every camper's best friend, and is suitable for all camp occasions. A warm woolly (or two if possible) is also a 'must' as late evenings and early mornings can be chilly even in the hottest weather.

Staff

The Guider in charge will have delegated duties before camp. Care must be taken, once delegation is made, not to interfere, except when the welfare of the girls or the equipment is at stake, or a valuable opportunity to give some acceptable training occurs. The aim of the staff is to work together as a happy team, helping each other out, and having fun together themselves. The attitude of the staff to each other and their general spirit is very quickly rubbed off on the girls.

Visitors' Day

Companies often arrange for the camp to be open for an afternoon so that parents and friends can visit the girls. This can be a valuable experience, as it gives the girls an opportunity to show, generally with great pride, what they have been doing and can do. Patrols enjoy entertaining their visitors to tea (but Q.M. usually has a large kettle of water boiling on the central fire in case the visitors exhaust any Patrol's resources). Some Companies like to put on an entertainment, show off collections, etc. It is wise to state in advance the exact hours when the camp will be open, and to discourage visitors from coming armed with hampers of sweets. A simple supper and a vigorous, hilarious programme might well be planned for that evening, after the visitors depart.

The Strike

If girls are trained in what to do, and a plan of action is made, striking camp is a quick, smooth operation, with Guides fully occupied and Guiders' tempers unruffled.

The less experienced the Guides, the earlier you start. On a week's camp you will probably want to start striking the day before you depart, especially if leaving before lunch-time. For a week-end camp, however, this would be rather unrealistic.

Patrols will be responsible for their own tents and kitchens, and the Patrol Leaders' Council will decide on the sharing out of other jobs—by volunteering rather than delegating! Rangers will probably establish a pattern with each having her own particular job. Guiders, unless totally inexperienced, will just get on with it.

Advance Striking

This might include:

Rubbish burning—Patrols should be responsible for their own.

Sorting out of stores and preparing the packed meal for last day (see Chapter 5).
Cleaning pots, etc. no longer required.
Striking marquee, some wash cubicles, spare tent.
Part-packing kit.
Dismantling gadgets.
Paying bills and 'thank you' visits.

Final Striking

1. Tents should be looped up so that they dry as quickly as possible. If rain threatens, put the kit in one tent (the easiest to dry off) and strike the others while dry.
2. Breakfast smartly, Guides, if possible, having kit and bedding packed.
3. Guides then complete striking kitchens, filling in fireplaces when cold, etc., leaving tents until dry.
4. Have hot water bin on central fire for washing of utensils, etc. required at the last minute. It can then be transferred to four bricks while central fire cools off and is filled in. The water will keep hot enough for needs.
5. Leave one toilet available as long as possible, giving warning, strike, and fill in the pit.

   (Time challenges, with an efficiency check at the end, can help the Guides to get going over striking.)
6. Meantime, general striking according to plan is going on, and well-trained Guides will lend a hand to other Patrols when they have finished their own tasks, or will see other jobs they can do to help.
7. Equipment should be checked for secure packing, especially if going by rail. Extra rope should be brought (it tends to disappear during camp). Hints on tying poles, etc. are given in Chapter 4. Equipment and kit can be sorted into piles for convenient loading.
8. A last clean up and freshen up of persons (a tin of freshening pads is useful if there is no stream). A last check that nothing, absolutely nothing, has been left to show you have been there ('except your thanks' as B.-P. said).

9. Many Companies like to finish by taking down the Colours with a simple ceremony and perhaps singing Daylight Taps.

It is worth remembering that in a really well-organised camp the participants should be blissfully unaware that they are being organised. Things go smoothly because people know what to do. The language of really happy organisation is not 'you do this' but 'who'll do this?', 'what about . . .?' and 'let's. . .'

Chapter 9.

CAMP ACTIVITIES

Tents to go up and down, stores to order, health to safeguard, gadgets to make and the pig bucket to empty—there is so much to think of, so many things, it would seem, to do, that it is possible to get them out of proportion and see them as being 'camp'. But the mass of hints and suggestions preceding this chapter are intended precisely to make this chapter possible. By aiming at maximum efficiency in all camp administration and chores, you ensure thereby maximum possible time for the things that camps are meant for: adventures, exploration, discoveries, ploys great and small, and, above all, fun, especially the fun of finding your own amusement at no expense. A really successful camp is one where no-one has missed the transistor radio, the local café, or any laid-on entertainments which seem to have become so essential to modern life.

Lay on a good programme for them? It really depends on *how* you lay it on! A completely Guider-inspired programme may work if it is something that catches on, but it can fall completely flat. In any case that would defeat all that we are aiming at in the Guide Movement. We must, somehow, impel the girls into laying on a good programme for themselves. How? Where they have no experience to build on by channelling their thinking in the right direction, by giving them a choice and by teaching them to select ideas from their Handbooks and allowing these to grow into a full-scale exciting activity, and, with newer campers, by whetting their appetites with challenges until they are ready to make their own.

'Can we please not have a camp challenge this year?' asked P.L., adding quickly when she saw dismay on her Guider's face,

'Last year's was super, but it's just that there's so much we want to do, there won't be time for a challenge as well.' The Guider's dismay turned to satisfaction. The Company had progressed and was ready to programme itself.

This does not mean that the girls want or need to be left to it entirely. There is an important place for the unexpected challenge—ideas for these there are in plenty in *A Handbook for Guiders* (*Guide Section*)—to keep the girls on their toes. The wise Guider learns to watch her girls and sense when they are happiest programming themselves, and when the moment has come to put on something which she knows will satisfy their conscious and unconscious needs.

Pre-camp and daily meetings of the Patrol Leaders' Council will ensure that the programme is being geared to their needs and desires.

Ranger camps will probably have had much more specific pre-camp planning of programme, but regular assessment of how it is working out can be helpful.

Guiders' camp programmes will depend on the purpose of the camp, and this should be kept in mind when planning is done. Valuable time, which might be spent in inspiring activities, should not be wasted on training in skills which do not require a camp setting.

Choosing and Using the Site

What the girls plan to do at camp will have determined the choice of site (see Chapter 3). Once there, it would be a great pity not to exploit its potential to the full and plan genuine out-of-doors activities, rather than bus-trips, shopping expeditions, etc., which are unrelated to a camp setting. If the girls themselves are slow, through lack of experience, to see the opportunities, offer a selection of activities for them to choose from, thus impelling them to make good use of the site, but leaving the ultimate choice to themselves.

Using the Site

Explore far and near. If exploring far, the girls should have practised walking and have the correct equipment, stout walking shoes, etc. Expeditions should have a purpose: visiting a historic ruin or building; following a map; tracing a stream to its source; making a dawn trip to see the sun rise; going on a night walk just to see what it is like at night, etc. These are just starters. The less-experienced will enjoy a quiz that will make them keep their eyes open on the way. Discovery can play a large part in these activities: something quite simple like 'What do cows do with their legs when they lie down?' or watching local farmers, fishermen, craftsmen, etc. at work (with their permission, of course).

Wide Games and Treasure Hunts

Using local legends and places of interest as a basis, these are popular: smugglers or pirates near the sea; cattle stealing in moors or woodland; sheltering an escaping general near a battlefield, etc. Local people are sometimes delighted to help. Surprise can play an exciting part in such activities: a message delivered by a stranger, or by post; sealed orders to be opened at a certain time, etc., can make an exciting start to a game. It is important, however, if the games take them far afield, that individual Guides do not go off alone, and that a latest time for return is fixed.

Pioneering Projects

The site will usually lend itself to some pioneering projects: a stream requiring a bridge; trees just made for a Patrol home to be reached by rope ladder; a pond on which a raft may be floated, etc. If planning this sort of project, it may be necessary to take with you some of the equipment: ropes, stout poles, etc., and also some sacking, which should always be used to protect trees when attaching ropes to them. *The Guide Handbook* has some ideas for this, For the more ambitious projects the list of books in the Appendix will be found useful and can be studied before going to camp. Pioneering is a popular activity for joint camps with the Scouts, and is a field in which they can help a lot. It is important that the results of pioneering labours should really be used, and not just constructed as an end in themselves.

Haymaker's bridge

Orienteering

Orienteering, along with other map-reading and compass activities, is another interest that can be the follow-up of pre-camp training and practice. It gives an ideal opportunity to try out, in new and unknown territory, the skills learnt on well-known home ground when practice is so often unrealistic. This is another popular joint activity, and if, as a result of joint training, an Orienteering camp is requested it shows the ideal state of affairs.

Bathing and Boating

If camping near a spot where bathing is possible, it would be a pity not to take advantage of this, especially if girls come from a place where opportunities to bathe are few. Before embarking on plans for bathing, however, it is essential to study the *Safety*

Rules leaflet. Bathing with other people's children in a strange place is a big responsibility, so certain steps to ensure safety must be taken. These are outlined in the leaflet.

The grade of the proposed site for bathing should be known (the local C.A. will tell you) and a life saver with the appropriate qualifications and not less than 16 years old must be present. (See *P.O.R.* 1973). So, to prevent possible disappointment, it is important to secure the services of an appropriately qualified life saver in good time.

Bathers should be divided into groups, each with a person who has a watch, lifeline, and some means of recalling bathers (a whistle is not always effective by the sea). First bathes should be short, limits clearly defined, obedience to orders insisted on, ducking and other horseplay and screaming forbidden. Bathing should not, of course, take place within two hours of eating a heavy meal, or when the girls are overtired, overheated, or unfit.

Sea Bathing

Never underestimate possible dangers of tides, currents, etc., and seek advice from local experts. It is often unwise, even for a strong swimmer, on an apparently calm day, to go beyond her depth.

Beware of: steep shelving shores, where there is a backrush of water; shores with sudden dips; submerged rocks; currents near rocks; seaweed, mud, and quicksands; pollution from a sewer.

Lake and River Bathing

Beware of: sudden shelving holes, eddies and currents, weeds, tins, broken glass, water pollution.

Boating

Rules for safety when boating are given in the *Safety Rules* leaflet, the details also appear in *The Ranger Guide Handbook*.

Observing Natural Life

How can we introduce the girls to the fascination of the natural life around them and perhaps spark off a new interest? What a pity it would be to miss the opportunity that camp gives. The

Handbooks give many starters which the girls should be encouraged to exploit to the full. Challenges can be adapted according to surroundings, whether woodland, moor, or shore with perhaps a choice of presentation, e.g., collection, log book, nature museum. Any visible end product will encourage the less enthusiastic. Challenges can be given to discover the most beautiful, or the most marvellous, to record observations from day to day, etc. A Guider's interest in their discoveries, and reference books to look up together, will all help to awaken and encourage an awareness of the things around them.

Using Natural Objects Creatively

This may be the doorway to nature for many girls, and in any case, in itself, affords great satisfaction. It may be producing a floral decoration, a hat for a Camp-Fire item, a spray for a visitor; making a picture of pressed leaves, grasses, or leaf prints; making shell figures or charcoal sketches; taking photographs; carving or whittling; or making dyes. Ideas can be inspired by the Handbooks, or sparked off by a challenge or specific need (Fig. 82).

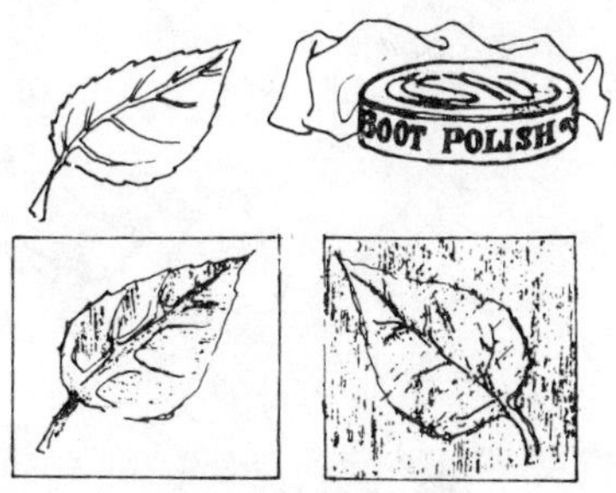

Fig. 82
With a cloth spread boot polish on underside of leaf. Place on paper and rub with another piece of paper to leave impression

Wet Weather Activities

As it does sometimes rain in camp, plans should be made for using this time in a way that will make everyone almost glad that it is raining! Many of the creative activities mentioned in the previous paragraph are very suitable for wet weather, and it is so much better if handcrafts are of material found on the site, and do not require much that has to be brought specially. Some drawing paper, felt pens, charcoal, sellotape, and glue will probably be sufficient bought material to keep everyone happy. Patrols can also plan and rehearse Camp-Fire items, make up camp poems and songs, or invent quizzes, challenges, etc., for each other. Outdoor activities are, of course, part of the wet weather programme too—provided everyone is appropriately dressed.

Miscellaneous Activities

Companies often have in camp certain events which the girls insist on every year, such as camp sports with unconventional events, e.g., Patrol-legged race, throwing the tin plate, potato and ladle (hooked on belt) race, or a Miss Camp Contest. Other events can be sparked off by a chance remark, e.g., an official opening for the refuse pit, a special launching ceremony for the raft, or the opening of the new bridge. Girl-inspired and girl-conducted they will be a howling success. Some have found a camp magazine successful. If the girls, throughout the year, are encouraged to be inventive, they will more readily have such brain-waves.

Camp-Fire

There is a very special atmosphere about a Camp-Fire in the twilight, which links the camp-fire circle very closely, intensifying the feeling of fellowship, sharpening perceptions, and generally creating a glow of well-being at the end of a day well spent.

A special site with a view (and not too conducive to midges) should be chosen, and turf taken up to leave a good space round the fire. Quick-burning woods, e.g., fir and other resinous woods, which give a good flame and not too much smoke, should be chosen for preference, and a good supply stacked near enough to be handy but out of the way of flying sparks.

It is sometimes worth while practising or learning songs before camp, or perhaps at elevenses, so that the girls can have that wonderful satisfaction of a beautiful song, well sung in lovely surroundings. Rounds and two-parts songs sound particularly well out-of-doors. Action songs and jingles give variety, as do word and action games and yells. Musical instruments, made in camp, can add zest to the singing. For Companies that like movement there are dances and singing games. Original stunts and parodies on camp life are much funnier than stale old ones. Songs that might give offence or embarrass should be quietly discouraged, e.g. comic parodies of serious songs, or songs which treat serious things in an offensively flippant way. The atmosphere of the Camp-Fire lends itself to stories and yarns, both grave and gay, from both Guider and Guide.

Evening Camp-Fires should always end on a quiet note. Some Companies, indeed, have their own special beginning or ending ceremony for Camp-Fire. Others end with prayers, a vesper, and perhaps Taps.

Whatever the programme, it should be the best the girls are capable of giving.

Service to the Community

Girls often feel that this is the most satisfying way of living up to their Promise, and welcome an opportunity for doing a Good Turn in camp. The local farmer may be glad of a helping hand, or some service to the nearest village may be appreciated: helping to clear a neglected churchyard, weeding an old couple's garden, clearing litter from a beauty spot, organising games for the local children, etc. Look for a need and act. Service projects should not be manufactured but should come as a result of a need expressed or seen.

Special Interest Camps

It can be very satisfying to be able to meet together, live in camp, and engage in some special interest: music making, acting, dance-drama, puppetry, handcrafts, bird-watching, pony-trekking, geology, archaeology, ski-ing, skin diving, water ski-ing, etc. Sports where special techniques and an element of danger are involved should only be contemplated with a qualified expert in attendance, and where applicable, e.g. mountaineering, only if the participants are physically fit.

The special interest may be service, and the suggestions in the previous paragraph may be found relevant. Projects must be chosen with care and might include such things as: helping out in homes to give staff a holiday; laying a Nature Trail in a popular camping or holiday centre; repairing storm or flood damage; clearing ground, or helping a remote village; providing staff for a play centre for children of working mothers during the school holidays. Each project must be worked out and proved possible before a promise is made.

Country Code

All Guides and Rangers should be brought up in the Country Code and should know to:

1. Guard against fire risks: keeping fires clear of bushes and low-hanging branches or anything else inflammable, such as dry grass in summer; being careful of peat and pine roots, which can carry the fire underground; soaking the embers and replacing the turf, if it has been removed, when the ground is cool.
2. Leave gates as they find them, and keep to paths when crossing farmland.
3. Avoid damage to fences, walls, etc. and not remove dead wood from hedges.
4. Keep dogs under control.
5. Leave no litter, and when possible remove any which others have left and which might do harm to people or animals.
6. Avoid disturbing sheep, especially in the lambing season. Report any animals in apparent difficulty or straying on a fenced road. (A sheep on its back should be set on its feet again.)
7. Be careful not to pollute water supplies, streams, etc.
8. Respect the life of the countryside. Wild flowers, etc. should be left for others to enjoy (one specimen for a collection is enough). Respect nests, plantations of young trees, and carve no initials anywhere.
9. Respect private property.
10. Leave the countryside as they find it (or even better).

Adventurous Activities

All Guiders, Rangers and Guides taking part in adventurous activities, e.g. ski-ing, water ski-ing, skin-diving, sub-aqua swimming, mountain activities, rock-climbing, caving, pot-holing, rifle-shooting, horse-riding, must observe the Safety Rules laid down by the Association.

Safety on Mountains

Any group contemplating hill-walking, mountaineering, etc., must know exactly what is involved, what rules must be obeyed, and adhere to them. They are under the following headings:

1. Training and knowledge.
2. Clothing and other essential equipment.
3. Route planning and leaving a note of the route.
4. Conduct of party on hills.
5. Acting in emergencies.

The booklet *Safety on Mountains*, published by the Central Council of Physical Recreation, or some other officially sponsored guide, must be read by anyone attempting such an activity. Countless lives are lost each year on our mountains as a result of ignorance or thoughtlessness.

Conclusion

The mark of a good camp? One that a girl has approached with zest—as a result of planning and preparation—and leaves feeling enriched in mind and body, with a feeling of achievement, of widened horizons and new interests, and the happy fellowship that comes from doing things together.

Chapter 10

THE PROMISE IN CAMP

Washing up, admiring the sunset, not screaming when a spider takes a fancy to your groundsheet, making a towel rail, hitting in a peg for the fourth time to get the guyline straight—these actions are all part of keeping the Guide Promise, as are all our actions. Somehow, however, the whole atmosphere of a Guide camp, the heightened perceptions, the sense of fellowship, the knowledge that we are doing this as Guides, can help us to be more aware of the fact, and this can be the golden opportunity to help Guides to see that, in *all* their actions, they can be living the Promise.

The 'Atmosphere' of Camp

Overheard: Two Guides, carrying their Patrol box across the site, to another Patrol:

'Wait till we have dumped our box and then we'll fetch yours'.

Pause, then one to the other:

'Gosh, you wouldn't think we were Guides to hear us. We should really have fetched *their* box first'.

Another Guide, after a game of rounders:

'It suddenly occurred to us that Isabel is the kind that never gets asked first when teams are chosen, so we picked her first, and you should have seen her face. And she really played well, too. It makes you think, doesn't it?'

Camp often sparks off that growing awareness of what it is about, what it means being a Guide, living unselfishly and thoughtfully. But does it always connect up in their minds, especially at Guide age, with the Promise and Duty to God?

The infection is easily caught and affects their attitudes, but girls of Guide age rarely use argument or even much deep thought to reach conclusions about religion.

'You know I never really "felt" religion until we went on that dawn hike and sang "The Lord's my Shepherd" on top of the hill', said one Guide. To have caught the infection is very valuable, but how much more valuable it would be if it helped them to realise that this attitude of unselfishness is part of their Duty to God, that this feeling should be an inspiration to act, that they must think about it and relate it to action, if these feelings and attitudes are to have any follow-up.

Yarns at Camp-Fire provide the opportunity and a setting conducive to stirring their thoughts. An activity can impel them into opening their eyes to the work of God's hand in the world: discovering the beauties and wonders of creation, doing a secret Good Turn to another Guide (perhaps one they don't like so much) and quietly analysing their own reactions; the Handbooks provide many 'starters' and ideas for this sort of thing. A quiet question relating the Promise or Law to a particular incident brought into conversation over chores or on a hike, a chat in the dark round the fire, when it is often easier to speak your thoughts; these are all ways of making use of a natural situation to show what the Promise is all about. Preaching in any form or a special 'pi' voice will have little effect. The most effective setting for letting the girls experience and realise the part God plays in their lives, however, is at camp prayers.

Prayers

Prayers in camp that really have meaning can be an enriching experience for all concerned. This communal act of worship can deepen the fellowship of the camp as well as touch individual minds and hearts. There may be girls whose particular denomination expects them to hold their own prayers and opportunity and encouragement must be given them to carry out their duty in this way. Otherwise prayers may be conducted with the whole Company, or Patrols may prefer to have their own prayers in the morning and join together in the evening. Some like to start the day with prayers, others find that pre-breakfast apathy does not produce the most receptive frame of mind and have prayers after breakfast chores are complete.

The Patrol Leaders' Council will no doubt decide whether the girls wish to conduct prayers themselves or whether they would prefer the Guiders to do it. The Rangers will probably choose to lead them themselves. While the experience of taking prayers can be an extremely valuable one to the girls, it is something with which, initially, they will need some help, especially if still of Guide age, but once a tradition is started and they find they can do this naturally and without too much disturbing self-consciousness, it is a very enriching experience.

It would be wrong to use prayers as a means of getting at people and deliberately putting wrongs right. On the other hand readings and prayers which do not relate closely to the experience of the girls, or which consists of a succession of religious phrases beyond their comprehension, are in fact worse than nothing. 'A lot of mumbo jumbo!' one teenager was heard to say after a particularly obscure oration. 'That's not for me.'

A book such as William Barclay's *Prayers for Young People* or, for the older girls, *A Plain Man's Book of Prayers* by the same author, makes an excellent starter. The prayers relate closely to day to day living in all its acts and relationships, and make very plain and telling the part God can play in the conduct of that daily life. Thanking God for the happy hike, survival after a stormy night, or the lovely singing at Camp-Fire, asking for strength to perform some difficult task cheerfully, courage to face spiders, or even forgiveness for burning the custard, will mean much more to the girls than highflown, religious-sounding platitudes.

Readings and prayers should be short. The longer they outlive the attention-span of the girls, the less meaning they will have.

Church Attendance

It is the duty of the Guider to see that every girl not only has the opportunity to fulfil the obligations of the denomination to which she belongs, but also is encouraged to do so. The booklet *The Religious Policy of the Girl Guide Movement* should be studied, particularly when girls of different denominations are in camp, and no girl taken to a service of another denomination without her parents' consent. Local clergymen should be contacted before camp and told of your proposed visit to their church. Many will also welcome an invitation to visit you in camp.

Guides Own Service

Camp is the ideal setting for a Guides' Own Service, but it must not be thought of as a substitute for a church service, but rather as a complement to it. There is no set pattern for it, and the girls, with or without help according to their wish and experience, will work out the form of service which appeals to them most. It may be traditional, or completely unconventional; it does not matter provided it is conducted in a spirit of reverence. Where girls belong to different denominations it is perhaps wise to ensure that the service is not biased towards the form of worship of one particular denomination in such a way as to make those of another denomination feel bewildered and embarrassed.

The choice of a particularly beautiful setting can make a Guides' Own Service an even more moving experience for everyone.

The Guider

In camp the Guider's example is on view 24 hours a day, and this is quite a salutary thought. The shared experiences bring Guider and Guide much closer, so her attitude to all things is bound to rub off in some way upon the girls. Her refusal to accept second-rate performance, her cheerfulness when things go wrong, her concern for others in mind and spirit, above all her own religious conviction—all these can unconsciously affect the girls and help them to grow.

The Guider, too, has an opportunity to get to know each girl better, to let her feel she expects the best of her, to show she trusts her, to stretch her according to her potential. By caring for each individual in her charge in the way that camp makes possible, the Guider can experience a very real and justifiable satisfaction in the knowledge that here is an opportunity to carry out her own Promise and to serve God in her loving care of his children.

Chapter 11.

HAPPY HOLIDAYS

What is a holiday? In Guide administrative terms, if you take a group of girls away from home and stay in some building, i.e., not under canvas, that is termed officially a 'holiday'. Before making promises to her Unit, a Guider contemplating running such a holiday should check with her Handbook and Commissioner that she has the appropriate qualifications.

Pack Holidays

The introduction to living communally as Guides is often made in the Brownie Pack when the Brownies go off with their Guiders on a Pack Holiday. Details of, and hints for, such ventures are given in the booklet *Pack Holidays*. Apart from being a valuable experience in itself, this is a good introduction to camp life and will help the Guide to adjust more quickly to living with others under camp conditions.

Guide Holidays

Holidays can be great fun for Guides and can provide an opportunity for them to enjoy aspects of the Eight Point Programme which cannot be experienced so deeply in any other setting. Living in a house can mean a much closer contact with other people than living in a field, and the give and take of relationships is experienced with much less chance of opting out. Adults and girls can get to know each other as individuals, and can see how one person inter-acts with another within the group. Conversation, in the kitchen, at table, and while doing chores and other activities, may become more meaningful, and develop into discussion on a level that is less likely in shorter meetings.

All experiences can be seen to be inter-related and be integrated into the total life of the community, and concerns can emerge and be expressed in prayers or services. (A radio, or newspapers help to keep a sense of proportion and an awareness of what is happening elsewhere.)

In a house, especially in a well-furnished one, there are opportunities for home-making and house-keeping to a high standard. This includes not only the chores associated with family living, but also the consideration for others which is necessary for harmony in any home. Courteous table-manners, the helping hand, the thoughtfulness that springs from a sense of the caring community—these will develop if the Guiders are ready to recognise and use the opportunities which arise from this situation.

On a holiday certain arts can be explored which are less practical on a camp-site where paper and materials can easily be broken, lost, or become damp and creased. Singing and other music-making, acting, etc., are as much fun round the sitting-room fire as the Camp-Fire.

If everyone takes some non-uniform clothes, 'changing for supper' can be tried occasionally, and this helps the girls' pride in appearance to be extended beyond wearing uniform correctly.

Although holidays are held indoors, there is ample scope for enjoying the out of doors, and, indeed, quite adventurous activities can be undertaken, even in bad weather, when there is a roof to come home to. This gives the Guiders and girls a greater sense of security, and early-morning adventures, night activities, or late night expeditions, can be indulged in without anxiety.

Service projects can also be undertaken on holiday, and surveys or special studies can be made more easily than in camp, but however enjoyable and instructive a holiday is, there is nothing in it that can replace that vital ingredient of camp—the contact, co-operation, and sometimes combat, with nature and the elements.

Ranger Holidays

These can play a large part in the Ranger programme and often provide a more suitable setting than camp for a full programme. They give endless opportunities to try out skills learnt, learn new ones, enjoy new experiences, and new places—in fact, generally to widen horizons, geographically, physically, mentally, intellectually, and spiritually.

The Purpose

The purpose is not merely a vital ingredient in the planning, it should be the inspiration of the holiday—an inspiration on the part of the girls (even though it may have been a slightly 'Guider-prompted' inspiration to help girls with little experience).

'We thought it such a good idea to take these country girls for a sight-seeing holiday in the city, but most of the time they were bored', said a Guider.

What went wrong? Could the right approach have made the same holiday a success?

'The girls did not enjoy their week-end at the youth hostel. They could not find anything to do and there were no shops', said another Guider.

What was missing? A purpose! The holiday, to be a success, should be the follow-up, the climax, indeed, of a period of exciting preparation, or the planned introduction to something new the girls wish to try out.

Out-of-Doors Pursuits

There is a wide variety of activities under this heading and some ideas may be found under Camp Activities in Chapter 8. These may include walking, nature study, orienteering, pony trekking, archaeology, canoeing, ski-ing, etc. (It is imperative when indulging in such sports as ski-ing, rock climbing, etc., that adults fully qualified in these pursuits are in charge of the girls and that the Safety Rules laid down by the Association are observed).

Where can you stay to pursue such activities? There are the Guide Outdoor Centres as listed in the Appendix. Many Education Authorities have Outdoor Centres which are available for Youth Organisations and information can usually be had from the appropriate Youth Organisers. Other centres, huts, etc., owned either by Guide groups or privately, are frequently advertised in *Guider* and some Pack Holiday houses are available off-season or at week-ends during term time. Field Study Centres run courses and Youth Hostels (see Appendix for addresses for Youth Hostel Association) make ideal centres for week-ends (a three-day maximum stay is usual) and special arrangements can be made for parties. The Guide 'grapevine' in Guider or Ranger and Guide circles can often produce the name of a suitable centre, and indeed may provide the inspiration for a new experience.

Indoor and Cultural Pursuits

The purpose of the holiday may be either to get together to pursue some common interest, e.g., music-making, folk dancing, studying architecture, or to take part in sightseeing, to visit museums, galleries, etc., or theatres, to pursue some historical or geographical survey, or perhaps to take part in a service project. Some of the centres mentioned above may be suitable for these. In towns, schools, Guide huts and hostels are possible sources of accommodation. In London there are Olave House, Girl Guide Commonwealth Headquarters, or Baden-Powell House. (See Appendix).

Touring Holidays

Touring holidays, walking or cycling, and using Youth Hostels, are popular. In a busy holiday season it is advisable to book hostel accommodation, which means planning the route carefully and sticking to plans. Hitch hiking is not recognised by the Guide Movement and is not covered by the C.H.Q. insurance policies. Girls should be discouraged from indulging in this form of transport even on their private holidays, both from the safety point of view and the attitude of 'something for nothing'. This may be an instance when a Guider may have to exercise a carefully explained veto on a girl-planned project.

Preparations

Practical

Finding accommodation and what it offers, e.g., whether the sanitation, etc., is adequate. If the accommodation is not known to you and does not have a specific recommendation, visit it if possible, or if not ask the local C.A. to have the place vetted, especially from the point of view of desirability of locality (a school which turns out to be in the centre of a gang warfare area might limit activities somewhat—to put it optimistically!).

Feeding arrangements. If meals are not supplied, check facilities for cooking, equipment and dishes available, and find out names of suppliers.

Health. The wise Guider will make provision for minor ailments or accidents in the shape of a suitably equipped first aid kit. If strenuous physical activity is to be undertaken, parents should be informed and it may be wise to ask for a doctor's certificate of fitness for each girl. The Association's insurance policy covers most activities, but the Guider should enquire from C.H.Q. if she is in doubt. Any accident or illness requiring qualified medical attention should be reported immediately to C.H.Q. for insurance purposes.

Transport. This should be booked in advance. If travelling by a service bus in any great number, the appropriate bus office should be informed.

Finance. Costs should be estimated well in advance, as girls may wish to start a saving scheme for the holiday. Each girl should contribute a realistic fee, unless there is a case of real hardship. For some particularly expensive project, the girls may wish to undertake some money-raising effort collectively or individually. (It should be a real effort, made by the girls themselves, not something done for them. The holiday will then mean far more to them.)

Kit lists. Lists should be issued in time for girls to obtain any clothes or equipment required. These will depend on the activities to be undertaken. Some Outdoor Centres have equipment available so check their lists first.

Joint holidays. If a joint holiday with Scouts is planned, it must be ascertained whether suitable separate sleeping quarters are available before embarking on the project.

Adult staff. The necessity for help and number of helpers required will depend on the type of arrangements, number and age of girls, and activities planned. Your Commissioner and C.A. will be able to advise you on this. If girls of Guide age are involved, and the Centre has no resident warden, a Guider must have another adult with her. On a joint holiday, there must be adequate staff for both sexes.

Programme

For outdoor activities, preparation will include increasing physical fitness, collecting suitable clothing, practising skills, finding out about the area. In addition, all participants should know the Country Code (see p. 125) and the safety rules relevant to their activity, e.g. *Safety on the Mountains* (see Appendix) for mountaineering and hill walking, *Safety Rules of the Girl Guides' Association.*

For activities of any kind, background reading, where relevant, will make the holiday much more interesting, and if skills or special knowledge are needed, these should be acquired. Libraries are an excellent source of information on many subjects and local experts may be flattered to be asked for tuition. Preparation for a holiday can form the basis for Company, Patrol, or group activities during the preceding weeks or months.

Girls who have trained themselves to notice things, who are always on the alert, who have learnt the satisfaction of trying out new things, will obtain maximum enjoyment from any holiday.

Organisation of the Holiday

Chores. The chores that have to be done will depend on the type of accommodation. Generally a rota system, as for camp, with Patrols or groups taking it in turn to perform the tasks required, will make for greatest efficiency. Rangers may prefer to select their duties and stick to them. Youth Hostels have their own method of allocating tasks to each hosteller every morning. Making beds, keeping the rooms tidy, respecting property, consideration for others, etc., will, of course, be expected of all Guides and Rangers.

Uniform. While an *esprit de corps* is easier to achieve when girls are in uniform, and the wearing of uniform when practical should be encouraged generally, there are pursuits for which it would be unsuitable, and Guiders must use common sense and discretion before insisting on it. When uniform is worn it must be neat and tidy and suitable for the occasion, e.g., jeans and shorts are not suitable for formal occasions, while to wear full uniform to climb a hill or clear litter from a lay-by would be foolish.

Programme. While the object of the holiday is to carry out the programme planned, free time must, of course, play a part and an opportunity given to enjoy in a social way the companionship of the others taking part. Neither in town or country will the girls want to go en masse the whole time. It can be very tiring and prevent the individual from following up her own interests. However, both in the heart of the country, when going far afield, and in large unfamiliar cities it is wise to make three the minimum size of group. Arrangements for going out at night will have to be very carefully made, according to the locality, and what parents would wish. Unfortunately, trusting the girls is not a sufficient safety precaution if the local youth cannot be trusted and girls meet situations beyond their experience (the limit of which they would not realise or be prepared to admit).

Joint Holidays

The most successful joint holidays with Scouts are those which are the natural outcome of shared training in some skill, e.g., ski-ing, orienteering, or are for the purpose of a joint service project, and are requested by the participants. These should have a fairly full, well-planned programme with the emphasis on the shared activity, which will give a good basis for such social activity as is planned. (Permission from your Commissioner is required before organising a joint activity of this kind. Such ventures, irresponsibly planned or run, could do much damage.) See also p.11. What has been said about joint camping also applies to joint holidays.

The Promise

As in camp, on a holiday where all the participants are learning to contribute to communal life, there is a wonderful opportunity for seeing the Promise in relation to life in all its aspects. The preceding chapter on The Promise in Camp will, of course, be as relevant to holidays as to camp. The notes on prayers, attendance at church services, and the Guides' Own Service should be read, as they apply equally to both.

A successfully run holiday, full of rewarding experiences, will provide inspiration and a pattern for many future holidays for the girls, whether as Guides or privately. By showing them how to gain maximum benefit and awakening their interest in all new experiences you will help to ensure happy holidays for them and their families throughout their lives.

Chapter 12.

HOLIDAYS AND CAMPS ABROAD

'Please, can we go abroad next year?'

That may be the question that launches a whole season's programme of pleasurable activity: planning, studying, listening and learning, making and working to raise money, etc. At the end will be a never-to-be-forgotten trip, a wealth of experience, a head full of memories and a host of new friends—the mind's horizon far extended and a new awareness that, despite superficial differences, people are basically the same the world over.

However, before that question can be answered, before 'operation going abroad' can be launched, the Guider must, to avoid subsequent disappointment, check with her Commissioner and County International Adviser that she may take girls abroad. It is a task that needs a measure of experience far beyond that of running a holiday or camp at home. She must, therefore, accept the judgement of those who know her, as to whether she is ready and trained for the task.

The County International Adviser acts as a link between the Guider and International Dept. at C.H.Q. and will be able to provide a great deal of help, information, etc. She will also supply the forms that have to be completed, information about insurance and other such practical matters.

Holidays

Planning and Administration

Long term planning is essential—about 6–9 months. Many arrangements have to be made. Accommodation and travel have to be booked and possibly money saved or earned by the participants.

Who is to go? The older girl (i.e. 14 plus) will gain most benefit from a party trip abroad. Twelve and 13 years old will certainly enjoy a trip but, in general, much more preparation will be needed to insure that they gain value from it. This could be done by careful briefing beforehand on what to look for and Quizes organised during the trip to open their eyes to all that is new. Otherwise their impressions tend to be based on known experiences and be directed more on such things as where to buy the best ice cream rather than how the cheeses are made.

Size of party. Small parties are preferable, about 20 being a good maximum. A larger party is recommended only if there are additional experienced adult leaders. The number of leaders will depend on their experience and on the size and ages of the party. A minimum of two adults for each party is essential, unless the group is of older and responsible Rangers.

Accommodation. *Where* will depend, of course, on the choice of the girls and what they are planning to do. *What* will depend on what is available there. Possibilities consist of Guide Houses (a list of these with addresses appears in the Appendix) or Youth Hostels. Write to the Youth Hostel Association (address in Appendix) for information about membership for parties and the address of the Y.H.A. in the appropriate country (the rule of three night maximum stay applies for most hostels). Some travel agencies dealing specifically with school and youth groups organise dormitory accommodation in hostels and schools at special rates. The headmaster or language teacher of your local Secondary School may be able to give you names and addresses of such agencies or lend you brochures. Advertisements in *Guider* may help you to find what you want. The Guide 'grapevine' is another excellent source of information about accommodation tried and tested, so keep listening and asking at Guiders' gatherings and ask your C.I.A. to link you up with Guiders who have already taken parties abroad.

Travel. This should also be planned well in advance. A reputable travel agency (choose one that is a member of A.B.T.A.), or one of the agencies specialising in youth travel mentioned above, can arrange this for you and will know the concessions available for group travel. They will also advise on the best route to take. If departure is from London, check that the time fits in with travel to and from your home town, with a safety margin for delays and transit through London.

Parents should, of course, be visited or met and the whole project explained to them. In some cases, and especially if the holiday is to take place in a high altitude, or if the girls will be engaging in strenuous physical activity, a doctor's certificate of fitness should be obtained.

Finance. As soon as possible, the exact cost of the holiday should be worked out, allowing for accommodation, travel, meals on the way, passports, charges for obtaining currency and travellers cheques, any additional insurance, excursions, etc. It is usually a good idea at some point in the negotiations to ask for a deposit. Many Guiders, too, find it a good policy to fix a maximum for pocket money. If money is banked as it is received (no doubt the girls will be saving over a period) you will have the benefit of the interest. A bank or travel agency can supply the required travellers' cheques—the best way of taking money abroad—though it is wise to arrange to obtain some ready currency in small denominations for immediate purchases on arrival.

Passports. Your local Post Office can supply you with a British Visitors' Passport which is valid only in Europe and for one year. Foreign Office passports are valid for ten years and available from your Regional Passport Office. If you decide to use a collective passport, information about these can be obtained from your Regional Passport Office.

Insurance. Your Commissioner or International Adviser will be able to supply you with information about the insurance coverage you automatically have when in charge of a group of Guides or Rangers. It is strongly advisable to extend the Medical expenses of the Headquarters Insurance Policy, because any medical advice or treatment needed abroad is very expensive. This extra cover can be arranged through the Insurance Department, C.H.Q. Any additional insurance you feel necessary, e.g., deposit due to cancellation, baggage etc., should be arranged at this point. If organising your whole trip through a travel agency, full insurance may be included in the cost.

Introduction Card. This is obtainable through your C.I.A. and is intended as a means of getting to know Guides in the countries visited. It is particularly useful for a girl travelling on her own.

Kit List. This should be issued in good time, so that girls have time to save up for, or make, anything new required. The list will depend very much on the climate expected (ask friends who have been there), activities planned, and the customs of the country. (In some countries the wearing of shorts or jeans in public is considered bad taste and there are places where bikinis are forbidden.) The choice will also depend on whether it is decided to wear uniform all the time or to wear mufti on certain occasions.

Preparation

However important it is to have soundly made arrangements to get there and back safely, and enough money to do so, etc., the efforts the girls make to prepare themselves are even more important.

The Purpose. To have any real value, a holiday abroad should have a definite purpose and systematic preparation.

'We got in a bus and stopped for ice-cream during the morning. We had horrible cheese sandwiches for lunch with the bread cut awfully thick, and then we went on for ages. At the hotel that night we had super chips for dinner'—was what one girl wrote in a school essay describing her holiday abroad.

What a lot of money wasted! To her the trip obviously had no meaning or purpose, she did not know what to look for, and her reactions were based entirely on existing knowledge, in this case food!

Older Rangers will already have specific interests, which will probably prompt them to go abroad in order to engage in further study, and they will try to choose the best country for following up their particular line. Outside help may be needed to guide them in their choice.

Many fifteen-year-olds will be more inclined to say 'Let's go to . . . this year!' If the Guider just goes ahead, organises all the details of the trip, takes them efficiently there and back, there is a danger that their reactions will be similar to those of the girl mentioned above and all they will be able to say is that they have been there.

The wise Guider will issue the challenge, 'But *why* do you want to go there?' which may prove the whole idea a waste of time and money, but will more likely impel the girls into seeing how such a trip could help them to follow up existing interests, acquire new ones, and give them an opportunity to see a different way of life. It may even lead them, when they start to think what they want to achieve by such a trip, to choose an entirely different country.

Thus their initial enthusiasm can be channelled so that a definite purpose becomes the prime motivating force, instead of some vague globe-trotting instinct, a purpose which requires definite preparation, such as that suggested below.

Preparation. If sightseeing is the basis of the programme, the girls will want to know what sights they are going to see. This they can learn by reading up about the country or district in travel books bought or borrowed from the library or friends. Those at school can ask information from appropriate teachers (who will be only too glad to respond to any such show of interest!). Maps of routes will be studied and some may suggest making and duplicating a set of maps so that each member has one, either a complete map or a blank one which she can fill up by herself. To know something of the history, geography, customs, etc., of the country will add tremendously to the interest of the trip.

If cultural visits, e.g., to museums, art galleries, ancient monuments are planned, some valuable homework can be done. Unless the girls have some tangible point at which they can start, the wealth of material in such places can completely befuddle the visitors. Corresponding places at home might be visited, so that comparisons can be made.

If walking, climbing, or some other physical effort will be required, muscles and limbs should be exercised in anticipation, and where possible the correct gear, e.g., boots, acquired and 'broken in'.

Getting used to the currency of the country is a help, doing some practice conversion sums, with money and also with weights and measures.

'If you wanted a pound of peaches, what would you ask for?'

One very valuable piece of work that can form part of the pre-holiday preparation is learning some of the language. Records such as Linguaphone are much more useful than a purely academic study of the language. Rangers who have left school may go to an Evening Class—classes in the spoken language are becoming more and more popular. If there is someone local who speaks the language, he or she may be able to help, and if not able to come to a meeting, may be willing to make tape recordings of useful phrases. If you are lucky, you could perhaps obtain the services of a teacher who has access to a language laboratory, and can plan a crash programme for you. Apart from the satisfaction and obvious practical advantage of being able to understand and make yourself understood, you will find when you get abroad that the local people will be so delighted to hear you trying to speak their language that they will very quickly become friendly. Many happy contacts are made in this way.

To visit a country and *not* meet the people would be such a waste that it just should not happen that way. All real friendships, however, consist of 'give' as well as 'take', so girls should be able to contribute to their hosts something from their own country, to speak about it, tell how things are done there, and be prepared to entertain them with national songs, dances, legends, recipes, crafts, etc.

Hints for the Journey

Tickets, etc. To avoid bitter experience the party leader is advised to keep all tickets for as long as possible, handing them out at the last minute if tickets have to be shown individually. Girls should be advised to have one safe place where they keep tickets, passport, money, etc., a place not accessible to the fingers of irresponsible neighbours in a crowd.

Movement. When the party is on the move (e.g. between trains) it is a good idea to have one adult responsible for bringing up the rear. With a very large party the best system is to allocate so many girls to each adult, for the sake of keeping together. It is much easier to keep together or spot missing members if the girls travel in uniform.

Luggage. Rucksacks, unless required for the activity planned, should not normally be used as they are awkward to handle in trains and buses and can be lethal in a crowd. They are not at all suitable for air travel. Suitcases or zip bags are easier to stow on luggage racks and to slip under beds. Girls should be advised to carry one case or bag with main necessities, and to have a haversack or duffle bag for items required on the journey, and to use for sandwiches, shopping, etc., when there. Girls may need to be reminded that they will be required to carry their own luggage, so perhaps a session on luggage-weight-reducing will not be out of place. Some travel agencies issue their own distinctive luggage labels, but if you are not enjoying this facility it is worth while making your labels distinctive in some way (and remember to pack some for the return journey).

Dress. Groups usually find it more practical to travel in uniform, as it makes for ease in keeping together as a party. (It can also have a psychological effect on conduct!) An exception to this might be if going ski-ing when perhaps uniform will not be worn at all. If uniform *is* worn it should be correct, complete, and tidy—for reasons which will be obvious. Guiders travelling abroad in summer will probably find the navy suit not practical and will opt for a cooler version of the uniform.

Food on the journey. If the journey is to be a long one, it is wise, if opportunity permits, to arrange for a proper meal on the way. A permanent diet of curly sandwiches and crumbling biscuits becomes less and less popular. Packed meals can often be ordered and picked up on the way, or meals vouchers for certain station buffets obtained. If food has to be carried, hard boiled eggs, wrapped cheese, etc., are preferable to elderly meat (which can be a health hazard). Crispbread, dates, raisins and chocolate also make good iron rations. Thirst is another hazard of travel and it is unwise to drink water at stations, etc. abroad. A provision of drinks is a good idea, in plastic bottles or in vacuum flasks (which will keep cool drinks cool). For the bad traveller: her usual supply of travel pills, dry biscuits, and boiled sweets to suck, can help to ease the situation.

Customs. A leaflet on what can be brought back is usually distributed to parties as they leave the country. It is helpful if girls, individually, make a list of their purchases to show to customs officials. Any concession with regard to bringing back wine or spirits does not apply to anyone under 18.

Miscellaneous hints. Face cleaning pads are very handy. Tissues have many uses, as napkins, in substandard toilets, etc.

Wear comfortable shoes. Feet swell in the heat. A scarf and extra woolly are generally advisable for a boat crossing. An air pillow helps to ease a long night journey by train. Misunderstandings may be prevented if girls know that there is not always segregation of sexes in sleepers or in toilets abroad, and that the latter may appear strange in form to them.

Organisation of the Visit

Each member of the group must realise that she is an ambassador for Guiding and for her country and that both may be judged by her conduct and appearance.

Thought for others. By practical application of the Law and Promise Guides can come to realise how their conduct in the various situations they meet abroad can be a revelation of their character. For example, new exciting experiences can make a group noisy, unless real consideration for others is ingrained. To ask 'How best can you keep the Guide Law in a foreign country?' is a better approach than a list of 'Don'ts'.

Dress. The girls will decide on what occasions uniform is to be worn. It may be all the time, or for some special occasion mufti may be more suitable. However, it must be one or the other, never a mixture. It is a good idea, in mufti, to wear the World Badge; many new friends are made through this symbol of World Sisterhood. As already mentioned, care must be taken to comply with local views on dress (no matter what other tourists are wearing).

Food. One of the major joys of foreign travel is the adventure of encountering new food—a joy, alas, denied some travellers because the wrong approach has been made.

'Maybe you won't like it' some misguided person perhaps said.

'Frogs legs' may have loomed large in some conversation. Perhaps they just lacked the courage to try something new, or the sense to try again something they did not like much the first time.

'I never used to like coffee', said one girl, 'but I'm really getting to like this French stuff'.

A psychological approach may be needed; the build-up of the wonderful food there.

'I hope we get some of their . . . They say it's marvellous'.

A tacit agreement that everyone must take a spoonful, at least, of everything unless it makes her ill, is usually very successful. Above all, give a reminder that lack of appreciation of food provided is an insult to those providing it, and as such is a breach of the Guide Law. That the Guiders show a good example in this, of course, goes without saying.

Chores. If these have to be done in hostel or house the work can be organised in a rota system as for camp. In addition girls will be expected to make their beds, and keep their rooms and common rooms tidy (as common courtesy and thought for others demand).

Pocket money. Many Guides prefer the leader or another adult to keep their pocket money and ration it out. Currency in small denominations is required for this.

Bathing and boating. The same safety rules as at home must apply for these. Study the *Safety Rules* leaflet before including these activities in your plans.

Sightseeing. Unless it is more economical because of special party rates to go as a whole group, it is generally better for girls to go about in small groups of three or four (not less). They will see far more, and achieve greater confidence, as well as having much more opportunity to meet and speak to the local people. Minimum numbers and supervision for evening outings will depend on the locality, and especially on the reputation of the local youth. Whenever girls are out in small groups, there should be a definite time and place fixed for their return, and girls should have with them a note of their holiday address.

Health. A tour or sightseeing holiday can be tiring, especially in hot weather. Often a rest after lunch, when the weather is hottest, is a good idea. Girls should wear scarves or sun hats in the sun, even if they do not need to do so at home. Sunbathing *must* be strictly limited. This is essential particularly by the sea or in high altitudes where they are not aware of how badly they are being burned. A first aid kit should be taken and should include calamine lotion for sunburn and Entero Vioform or similar tablets for tummy upsets. Enquiries should always be made as to whether or not the local water supply is safe for drinking.

Staff. If the staff share in such duties as are necessary and in all the planning it will be excellent training for all concernd as well as leading to a happy team spirit. At the same time, it must be remembered that it is a holiday.

Opportunity should be the basis of all day-to-day organisation of the holiday—to enjoy new experiences (and not just to go down to the swimming pool every day or to look at the local shops), to visit the places read about, to eat new dishes, to risk a ride in a cable car, to talk to the local people to look, listen, wonder and digest.

Conclusion

And after you get home, after all the 'thank you' letters are written, and the sun-hat is relegated to the attic, how much is left of the holiday? Did you keep a diary? It helps to fix impressions and keep experiences alive. Did you collect tickets, postcards, take photographs? Or did you just have memories? An illustrated log of your holiday compiled by the individual, group, or Company will make a lasting reminder of a wonderful experience.

Camps Abroad

These fall into different categories. One girl may go either as a delegate from her Country or to join a pen pal in camp by private invitation. A whole group or Company may go to join a Company abroad with whom they have some link. Or a Company may plan to camp independently in a foreign country with which they have no specific link, having heard or read about a suitable site.

A Delegate to a Camp

A girl chosen as a delegate, anyone going to mix with Guides of other countries, must obviously be a good ambassador for her own country, an upholder of the Guide Promise and Law, adaptable to a different way of life and different food (and prepared to enjoy them), impeccable as to uniform, interested and interesting—one with a spirit of adventure, one who will be a real friend to all whom she meets.

She should make careful preparations for her visit, by reading up about the country, finding out about its customs, etc., and at the same time making sure she will be able to interest her hostesses in her own country and teach them some songs, dances, or a local craft.

A kit list will normally be sent her, along with a note of any other requirements. If travel arrangements are not made for her, a reputable travel agency will do this.

A Group Camp Abroad

Most of what has been said earlier in this chapter on holidays abroad will be applicable and should be studied. As far as luggage is concerned, however, for camp softgrips or kitbags will be more suitable than suitcases. If the group is taking camp equipment as well and hands have to be free to carry a share of this, rucksacks may be recommended.

A high standard of camping efficiency is necessary as conditions can be very different from those at home. A large measure of adaptability is another vital ingredient of both party and individual make-up.

If camping as a unit on your own, get local advice on conditions, means of transport, shopping, possibilities, etc., and it would certainly be wise to have with you someone who can speak the language fairly well.

If touring and camping, for example by minibus, only official or privately owned camp-sites should be used. It is unsafe, and against the law in some cases, to camp just anywhere. Charges for such sites are small and depend on facilities available. If planning a tour through a motoring organisation, full information and the required 'carnet' can be obtained from them.

If camping with Guides of the country you may have to be ready to adapt quickly to their way of camping, with very different traditions, very different camp arrangements. The true Guide enters this experience in a spirit of enjoyment (never with a 'not so good as our way' attitude!).

When equipment has to be carried it should be lightweight and packed for convenient carrying. Transport arrangements that ensure the safe-conduct of equipment are essential and should be made early. It may be possible, at additional expense, to register it. If not you should make sure that you really can carry it all between you if necessary. Porters are sometimes scarce, and expensive.

Conclusion

If plans and preparations are well made, if each individual is trained to be a Guide, if the spirit of adventure is ever present, any trip abroad, whether a holiday or a camp, can influence a girl for life, broaden her outlook, and make her a better friend to all.

Chopter 13.

DAY CAMPS

Do we really ensure that all girls get an enriching out-door experience? What about the girls who, for various reasons, good or bad, never have the opportunity to go to camp? What about the girls who are not ready for a full-time outdoor life or who are denied it for some physical reason? A Day Camp provides the ideal situation for these girls to learn the fun of being in the out-of-doors and using its facilities. It should not, of course, be looked on as a substitute for camp. It is a different type of outdoor activity which could be regarded as a supplement to camp and, for some, as an introduction to it.

What Is a Day Camp?

The girls live at home and go each day to a site where they have a programme of activities based on the out-of-doors. As some sort of continuity and an opportunity to progress from day to day are vital to the success of a Day Camp, it should not be a single day's experience, but a series of days extending over a week or more, or, at the very least, two or three successive weekends.

Where Are Day Camps Held?

A Day Camp might be held at an established camp-site, thereby perhaps making fuller use of a good site than if it were limited to residential camping. While any site that is suitable for a camp will also be ideal for a Day Camp, a much wider field is open. In fact any place which offers scope for out-door activities is suitable, provided there are no potential dangers present. A wood, a sea-shore, some spot by a stream or a lake are obvious choices. But a Day Camp can equally well be held in a corner of a city park, a piece of waste ground, or even someone's garden. The three test questions are: Is there scope for real outdoor activity? Is it safe? Has permission been given to use it?

Who Goes to a Day Camp?

Day Camps are suitable for girls of both Brownie and Guide age. A Brownie Pack or Guide Company may well decide to run its own Day Camp, with a programme which is a follow-on of weekly meeting-time activities. A very successful Day Camp, however, can be organised at District, Division, or County level, catering at the same time, if need be, for both Brownies and Guides. Participants are divided into units no larger than a Pack or Company and grouped according to age, experience, and programme interest. Such a camp provides an opportunity to make many new friends. A very rewarding form of Day Camp can be run for under-privileged children, either on their own, or participating along with Brownies or Guides. Experienced Guides or Rangers may possibly run an ordinary camp and invite girls to join them by day to participate in their camp activities. Children whose mothers go out to work might also be invited to such camps during the school holidays.

Staffing a Day Camp

A Day Camp at District, Division, or County level is the responsibility of the appropriate Camp Adviser, and would be run by her, or someone delegated by her—someone with a real understanding of the programme possibilities of such a camp, and the administrative ability to handle the numbers that will be involved. A Unit Leader should be a Guider (or Commissioner) experienced in handling that particular age group and capable of getting the best out of the girls and the facilities. She should have at least one assistant, the number depending on the size of the unit and programme needs. Finding staff for a Day Camp may well present no great difficulty, as even Guiders who have home commitments may be available for the hours involved. Interested mothers may also be persuaded to help, especially if a special 'nursery' unit is set up in the Day Camp where younger children of staff members are catered for. Rangers too enjoy helping at this type of camp. For special interests, outside experts may well be brought in.

A wise Guider-in-Charge will see that staff receive pre-camp training appropriate to their function at the Day Camp.

A Guide or Brownie Guider proposing to run a Day Camp for her Unit must have the permission of her Commissioner and Camp Adviser before embarking on plans, and have the site approved.

Preliminary Arrangements

Preliminary arrangements for a large Day Camp consist of finding a site and staff, deciding on numbers and method of recruiting, deciding whether the programme is to be general or specific, working out what information will be required on camp forms and issuing these. At this stage the method of transport will have to be arranged and the cost of the camp worked out.

Nearer the time, girls will be divided into appropriate groups. Staff will be trained and assigned to groups. A rota of duties, where applicable can be drawn up, e.g. providing a colour party, care of toilets, taking prayers, etc.

Equipment

The amount of equipment needing to be taken will depend on what is available on the site. Day camps may be run, in fact with very little equipment. Provision must be made for toilets and hand-washing facilities. (See Chapter 6).

Some form of shelter for wet weather is also essential. At an established camp-site this may well be there already. It may be possible to arrange for the use of a nearby school or church hall. Marquees may be available or have to be hired. On a sheltered site, a large shelter, similar to a dining shelter (see Fig. 83) for each unit (with an area of approx. 6 m. by 6 m.) is worth acquiring if Day Camping is to be done to any extent. The canvas may be made to specification or might be devised from an old marquee

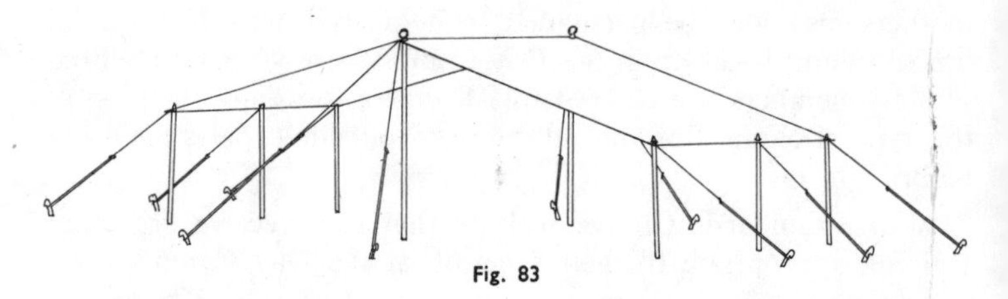

Fig. 83

roof. Large sleeping tents (ex-army or similar) might be acquired cheaply second-hand (they do not need to be one hundred per cent waterproof).

If cooking is to be included in the programme, the appropriate materials to make a fireplace, and utensils will be required (see Chapter 5).

Otherwise equipment required will depend on programme needs.

It may be necessary, depending on the Day Camp site, to arrange for safe overnight storage of equipment, or even to have it brought home.

Transport

Girls should receive written instructions about arrangements for transport. The easiest means of transport is probably by special bus. If the site is near a service bus route, the local bus company may be prepared to put on duplicate buses. It would be unfair for large numbers to use a service bus without warning the company in advance.

If using public transport, girls may need to be reminded not to allow their excitement and high spirits to become a source of annoyance to other passengers.

Long bus journeys to and from Day Camp should be avoided.

Health and Safety

At each Day Camp there must be an adult qualified to give first aid and a well-equipped first aid box must be available. (See page 90 for suggested contents.) There should be some provision made for a girl who feels unwell to lie down (e.g. groundsheet, air bed, and blankets) and some means for water to be boiled.

The First Aider should have worked out, in advance, the procedure in case of accident according to local conditions, remembering that girls, if possible, should be attended by their own doctors if they are within reach of them. (This will mean including the name and telephone number of the girl's doctor on the camp form.)

Safe drinking water should be available, even if it has to be brought in water carriers, and kept covered.

If bathing is included in the programme, the rules laid down in the *Safety Rules* leaflet must be observed. (See also pages 119-120.)

A note on Insurance Cover appears on page 30.

Meals

Possibly most valuable use can be made of the time available if girls bring packed meals with them, although it is a good idea to provide milk or squash. It may be, however, that cooking is an integral part of the programme either on a camp fireplace or hike fire, either for one day only or daily. Such meals will have to be budgeted for, before assessing the cost, or girls asked to bring the appropriate ingredients. (See Chapter 5 for details about menu planning, fireplaces, washing up, etc.)

Times should be set aside for eating, and in-between nibbling discouraged—as part of both health and social training.

Dress

Ideally girls should wear camp uniform (it has a psychologically good effect on behaviour) and efforts should be made to make this possible. If this is just not possible for financial reasons, girls should be encouraged to wear clean, tidy clothing suitable for the out-of-doors and the climate. It would be unrealistic to expect them to get full enjoyment from the programme wearing full uniform.

Kit List

The details will depend on the facilities of the site and the programme planned. Every girl, however, should be asked to bring wet weather wear, including a plastic mac (many anoraks are no more than showerproof), wellington boots, gym shoes or wooden soled sandals (these last two worn without socks in rain) depending on the ground conditions. A jersey should be brought if not already worn, and a sitter groundsheet. Probably food for the day will be required, but if cooking is to be part of the programme, appropriate dishes and cutlery should be brought. Programme needs will determine other items needed.

Preparation

Girls attending Day Camp should be encouraged to prepare for the experience by acquiring the skills they will require, learning the Country Code, making useful equipment, etc., so that they gain the maximum benefit from the experience.

Programme

A well-planned programme is not only vital to the success of a Day Camp, it is the very reason for having one.

A Company or Pack, going on its own, will use the Day Camp as the highlight or culmination of some planned project or projects, or may even use it as a 'starter' for a new one. This is an excellent opportunity to make the fullest possible use of the Patrol System.

In the larger Day Camp, incorporating girls from different Units, the girls should have as large a share as the set-up and activity allow, in planning and conducting the programme. A Brownie unit should set aside some time each day to come together and discuss the programme past and future. In Guide units, Patrol Leaders should be chosen by their Patrols as soon as possible, time should be given for Patrols to discuss together and a regular Patrol Leaders' Council should be held.

The actual programme may be a general outdoor one based on requests made on the application form or made by the girls in camp once they have seen the facilities. For girls who have little experience of Day Camps and their possibilities it may be found more practicable to present, initially, a selection of programme ideas from which they can choose.

However, a Day Camp may also be run for a specific purpose where a need, interest, or opportunity has presented itself. Several different specific activities might also be offered, the girls joining the unit with the activity which interests them most, either for the whole duration or changing round each day. While activities may change, units should remain the same so that the girls have a chance to progress in relationships within their own group.

The Guider-in-Charge will, of course, co-ordinate activities to ensure the best of the facilities of the site and prevent overlapping (such as three units all planning to cook on the same day on one fireplace!).

The choice of Day Camp activities is large. Ideas in the Outdoor Sections of the Handbooks provide an obvious programme choice, as do outdoor badges. Nature observation, exploration, whittling and other crafts using natural objects, making dyes, studying the seashore, river and pond life, sketching, photography, local history or archaeology, outdoor cooking, pioneering projects, wide games, orienteering, weather lore—possibilities abound.

Whatever the activity, it must be one the girl has chosen to do, not one to which she has been directed for administrative convenience! She must have the opportunity to participate (not just stand around and watch) and experience the joy of tackling something new and achieving something worthwhile.

The Result

For the girls the result of a well-run Day Camp will be a new awareness of the out-of-doors and what it can offer, a new zest for life, many new friends and a better understanding of others through having shared an exciting, challenging experience with them, and, of course, tremendous fun.

APPENDIX

The following properties are owned/administered by the Girl Guides' Association and are available to members of the Movement for camps and holidays. Application for information and bookings should be made to the booking agent and not to the site or centre. Addresses for bookings are given from time to time in *Guider*, and are also in the current *Camp Advisers' List* (issued annually to C.A.s) and *The Ranger Guide Handbook*.

Many Counties also have properties which are available to all members of the Movement for camps and holidays.

Camp Sites

Blackland Farm, Sussex (C.H.Q.)
Broneirion, Montgomery (Wales)
Brownsea Island, Dorset (C.H.Q.)
Chigwell, Essex (London)
Cudham, Kent (London)
Foxlease, Hants (C.H.Q.)
Lorne, Co. Down (Ulster)
Netherurd, Peebleshire (Scotland)
Waddow, Lancashire (C.H.Q.)
Ynysgain, North Wales (C.H.Q.)

Holiday Houses

Y Bwthyn Bach, Montgomery (Wales)
Chigwell Hostel, Essex (London)
The Colebrook Cottage, Co. Fermanagh (Ulster)
Cudham Hostel and Pack Holiday House, Kent (London)
The Irene McKibbin Memorial Cottage, Co. Down (Ulster)
The Margaret Pollack Guide Cottage, Co. Tyrone (Ulster)
Netherurd Pack Holiday House, Peebleshire (Scotland)
Restrop, Blackland Farm, Sussex (C.H.Q.)

Note: Pack Holiday Houses are available for Guides out of season.

London

Baden-Powell House (Scout Association)
Commonwealth Headquarters (G.G.A.)
Olave House (W.A.G.G.G.S.)

Adventure Centres

Drimmrie, Perthshire (Scotland)

Glenbrook, Derbyshire (England)

Lochgoilhead, Adventure and Boating Centre, Scotland.

European Guide Hostels

(For further information apply to your County International Adviser).

Belgium

Le Trait d'Union, Lince par Sprimont.
Domaine de Mozet, Mozet par Nameche.

Denmark

Det Danske Pigespejderkorps Pigespejderborps, Snekkersten.

France

La Nef, Paris.
Foyer International d'Acceuil et de Culture, Paris.
Holiday Centre de Bois d'Amor, Bois d'Amont.

Germany

Pfadfinderinnenheim, Immerhausen Pfadfinderinnenschaft St. George, Ammersee.

Luxembourg

Centre d'Accueil International, Luxembourg City.

National Training Centre Colpach.

Netherlands

N.P.G. Centrum Buitenzorg, Baarn.

Switzerland

World Guide Centre

Our Chalet, Adelboden, Switzerland.

Useful Addresses

Camping Club of Great Britain and Ireland, 11 Lower Grosvenor Place, London, S.W.1.

Central Council of Physical Recreation, 26 Park Crescent, London, W.1.

Youth Hostels Association, 29 John Adam Street, London, W.C.2.

For addresses in other countries of the United Kingdom see *A Handbook for Guiders R.G.S.*

For Travel Abroad

Association of British Travel Agents, 10 Mayfair Place, London, W.1.

BIBLIOGRAPHY

Camp Cooking (G.G.A.)
Quartermaster in Camp—E. Robertson
Notes on Camps and Holidays (G.G.A.)
Notes on Boating and Holidays Afloat (G.G.A.)
Safety Rules (G.G.A.)
What Every Guider Should Know about Insurance (G.G.A.)
Camping and Education (H.M.S.O.)

Lightweight and Mobile Camping:

Camp and Trek—Jack Cox (Lutterworth)
Camping and Hiking—Falcon Travis (Knight Books)
Help Yourself to Hike Cooking—P. Hollingum (G.G.A.)
Better Camping—Alan Ryalls and Roger Marchant (Kaye and Ward)
The Back Packers' Book—Derrick Booth (Hale)

Pioneering:

Pioneering with Patrols—(Scout Association)

General:

Know the Game Series:

Camping, *Map-reading*, *Orienteering*, *etc.* (Educational Productions)

Safety on Mountains and other booklets. (List on request.) (C.C.P.R.)

Mountain Rescue and *Cave Rescue* (issued by the Mountain Rescue Committee)

Expedition Guide—John Disley (Duke of Edinburgh's Award Office)

Prayers:

Prayers for Young People
The Plain Man's Book of Prayers
More Prayers for the Plain Man
} William Barclay (Fontana)

Prayers of Life—Michael Quoist (Gill & Son, Dublin)

The Religious Policy of the Girl Guide Movement in Great Britain (G.G.A.)

Various Books of Readings and Prayers (see current G.G.A. book list)

First Aid:

First Aid Manuals: St. John Ambulance Association
St. Andrew's Ambulance Association
British Red Cross Society

Miscellaneous

The Ranger Guide Handbook (G.G.A.)

The Guide Handbook (G.G.A.)

A Handbook for Guiders — Guide Section (G.G.A.)
— *Ranger Guide Section* (G.G.A.)

INDEX